Moraga Deconstructed: Illuminations in Mexican-American Heritage

By Nikolas Gonzales
Edited by Rob Bignell

"Moraga Deconstructed: Illuminations in Mexican-American Heritage," by Nikolas Gonzales. ISBN 978-1-947532-74-8 (softcover); 978-1-947532-75-5 (eBook).

Library of Congress Number on file with Publisher.

Published 2018 by Virtualbookworm.com Publishing Inc., P.O. Box 9949, College Station, TX 77842, US. ©2018, Nikolas Gonzales. All rights reserved. No part of this publication may be reproduced, stored in a retrieval system, or transmitted in any form or by any means, electronic, mechanical, recording or otherwise, without the prior written permission of Nikolas Gonzales.

For Grandpa...

Acknowledgements

FIRSTLY AND MOST IMPORTANTLY, I would like to thank you, the reader, for opening up this book. I really hope you enjoy and get something out of it.

Next, I would like to thank my lovely grandparents/guardian angels Lola and Eddie Moraga, Lupe Contreras, and Christopher Gonzales whose inspiration and guidance prompted me to write this book. I think about them all of the time. Still. Writing this has brought me closer to them than I ever thought possible and it has been incredibly hard to stop. Even now, I can feel them sitting by my side helping me do this, even if they are no longer with me.

I would like to thank my beloved wife Dr. Melinda Negron-Gonzales for also inspiring me to put this book together and put my obsession with history and travel to use. She has been the epitome of kindness and patience and has been an erudite example for me to follow. I could not have done this without her.

Thank you to my best friend Leif Hillesland for being an awesome listener, critic, and motivator. His enduring love for the pursuit of art continuously motivated me to write and research. His ideas and encouragement kept me going when I could do nothing but look at my computer, and bleed.

Thank you to all of the interviewees who contributed to this book, who just also happen to be part of my family too: my mother Rosalinda Moraga, uncle Edward Moraga Jr, cousin Cherrie Moraga-Lawrence, and grandfather Edward Moraga. I would also like to thank my grandmother, aunts, and uncle that did not participate but deserve mention: my grandmother Lola Moraga, my aunts Patricia Gonzalez and Anna Murphy, and my uncle James Moraga.

I would also like to thank the following organizations: Mission Dolores, San Francisco CA, San Francisco Presidio, San

Nikolas Gonzales

Francisco CA, Mission San Gabriel, San Gabriel CA, Moraga Historical Society, Moraga CA, The Santa Barbara Mission, Santa Barbara CA, The Tubac Historical Society, Tucson CA, Hernani City Hall, Hernani, Gipuzkoa, Spain, Palacio del Los Olvidados, Granada, Spain, Catedral de Santa María de la Sede, Sevilla, Spain, The Museum of the Battle of Navas de Tolosa, Santa Elena, Spain- Thank you to the staff for opening the museum for my wife and me on a Sunday when it was closed and taking the time to explain the complexities of the battle to us. For the countless hours I spent at Mr. Crepe in Davis Square, Somerville, MA, Boston Public Library, Boston, MA.

Thank you to the following people: Pam Meeds Williams, Nancy Holub Valentine, Mindy Maddock, Dr. Monica Orozco, Gustavo Polo, Sanjay Bansal, Yasmin Chassi, Ben Beardsley, Erin Katie Bartels, Jose Atiles, Ruary Allen, Frank X Moraga, Calango, Sucuri, my editor Rob Bignell, my parents Linda Moraga and Frank Gonzales, my step-mother Dorothy Gonzales, my inspiring sister Dr. Renee Marquez, brother-in-law Manny Marquez, my brother Daniel Moraga, sister-in-law Sisily Moraga, my nephews E.J. and Noah Marquez, and my niece Daphne Davis for her encouragement, my in-laws "The Negrons," my cousin Erik Garcia for steering me in the right direction with my writing and publishing, DLT- you know how you are, Mark Pijanowski for the media help, Rhianon Gutierrez for your opinions and proofreads.

Lastly, thank you to anyone I missed. I know you're out there so forgive me.

Table of Contents

Chapter 1 Conversations at the Kitchen Table 1
    Before We Begin… 2
Chapter 2 The Moor Expulsion 5
    Spain in the Medieval Period 5
    Pre-Medieval and Medieval Spain 5
    Arias Moragas and the Battle of Las Navas de Tolosa 8
Chapter 3 The Inquisition and the "Moriscos" 11
    Spanish Unification 11
    Abduction and Secrecy 14
    Burned at the Stake 15
Chapter 4 The Caribbean Natives 17
    Martin De Moraga and Native Resistance in Caribbean ... 17
Chapter 5 The Mainland 21
    North American Conquest 22
    The Yaqi and the Mayo Natives 22
Chapter 6 Diversity, Marriage, and Property in Early Eighteenth Century New Spain 25
    Gender and Diversity in New Spain 25
    Rosa Texarra Moraga 26
Chapter 7 Eighteenth Century New Spanish Frontiers ... 28
    Jose Joaquin Moraga 29
    The De Anza Expedition and the Ohlone 30
    Jose Ignacio Moraga—The Apache in Pimeria Alta 32

Chapter 8 The 1800s 35
   Augustine Moraga – Mexican-American Union Soldier 35

Chapter 9 Mexican-Americans and the Labor Movements of Los Angeles 40
   The Mexican-American in the Twentieth Century 40
   Edward Moraga, Los Angeles, and World War II 41
   The Labor Movements of Los Angeles in Edward Moraga's Youth 42
   Back from the War 44

Chapter 10 The Contemporary Chicana Artist 46
   Cherrie Moraga Lawrence 48

Conclusion 51

Appendix 56
   Obstacles 56
   Reasoning 57

Bibliography 65

Endnotes 69

Chapter 1
Conversations at the Kitchen Table

GROWING UP IN LOS ANGELES, my grandfather would often tell me, "Mijo,[1] we are Mexican-Americans, but we are Californios." Being young and dismissive, with a sarcastic look on my face and puzzled by his sentence construction, I would reply, "Okay Grandpa..." and walk away thinking that what my grandfather, Edward Moraga, had just said was nonsense. "Of course we are Californios," I thought. "We live in California. *Hello?!*"

I mistakenly thought that my grandfather was using one of the Spanish interpretations of the term because of where we were born and where we lived. Little did I know that the historic interpretation meant something very different: "Californios" were also Mexican-Americans from what used to be the Alta California regions of Mexico, the present-day California and Arizona of the United States. In essence, my grandfather was telling me that our family had lived in California since it was part of Mexico, and possibly even before, when this area was a Spanish colony.

"Pappy" loved to talk about his history. I often found myself subjected to hour-long chats about World War II and his experiences in it while we all sat at the dinner table. Because I was young and didn't have any context for what Pappy was trying to tell me, it felt monotonous. I tried to ignore him but after a while, without realizing it, this tradition of oral histories made an impact on me. Looking back on those times, I am deeply thankful for having such a wise mentor, guide and friend to tell me about our past.

It was this "Californio" aspect of our family tree that inspired me to write the book you're reading now.

Nikolas Gonzales

When I eventually realized the truth about the type of primary and secondary education I'd been given, I could see there were holes in my understanding of my own cultural identity. I needed to know more about the Mexican side of my lineage and decided to look into the supposed extensive background of my grandfather's genealogy.

My grandfather's last name, Moraga, is not very common among Spanish surnames, but even as a young man, I remembered hearing that it was an *important* name in California's history, even though it was never formally taught to me. As I read more after college and graduate school, I became aware that my grandfather's family might have played critical roles in the development of California during the Spanish colonial period. The Moragas were some of the first European explorers to settle the West Coast in the late 1700s, while the British colonials were fighting for independence on the other side of the continent. The town of Moraga in northern California is supposedly named after my grandfather's family, and there are streets with the name Moraga throughout California.

As I reflected on all of this, I could see my public school education system had disregarded an important piece of American history. I could spot the gaps because what was missing was indeed my own *personal* history. The biases that I was essentially force-fed as a student had all but severed my connection with the lands of my supposed ancestors—even those that might be considerably more important than other, whiter, historical figures we did study. I decided to use my knowledge as a history instructor to embark on a journey into my grandfather's pedigree, to explore not only a theoretical genealogy for my own family but also to understand how these possible family members lived in their own times.

I stumbled during this process, changing my focus, digging deeper into history, but along this road I became enlightened in ways I never expected. I would like you to join me now while I share the story of the Moragas, as I came to know them.

Before We Begin...

IN MOST U.S. HISTORY BOOKS that cater to younger students in America, the first chapters usually involve lessons on the first

Englishmen establishing Jamestown in 1607 and eventually the Pilgrims arriving on the Mayflower in 1620 and constructing Plymouth Plantation in present-day Massachusetts. These two events were undoubtedly pivotal in U.S. history, but in my experience as both a U.S. and world history instructor and public education graduate who took U.S. history all throughout primary, secondary, and higher education, they promote a message that the British were the first successful European settlers in North America. Rarely is it mentioned that in the early 1600s North America had essentially become a free-for-all for many western European nations. The French were establishing themselves in Canada, and the Dutch were living in New Amsterdam in what today is New York City harbor. The Spanish and French had already founded cities in Florida in the 1500s and eventually went on to be so forward-thinking as to establish the first free city for slaves at Fort Mose hundreds of years before the American abolition of slavery. The Spanish were also moving toward settling what is now the U.S. Southwest during the early 1600s.

Even more disappointing in my experience is little to nothing is mentioned about the integral roles Native Americans, indentured servants, and African slaves held in social, economic and political spheres in budding New England. All too often, it feels as if the United States had come from an idea and into fruition on its own without the very necessary interaction with non-English governments and peoples. The United States always has been a multicultural society, but this is hardly ever touted or celebrated in the first chapters of U.S. history texts used in K-12 education.

Initially, my aim for this book was to research Jose Joaquin Moraga's lineage (one of the founding members of the San Francisco presidio in 1776), and like many genealogical studies, I planned to expound on the typical *excellence* of a patrilineal bloodline that spanned from Western Europe down through the centuries eventually to my grandfather Edward Moraga. I quickly saw that doing this would only be contributing to the same myopic, Eurocentric, and undoubtedly patriarchal narratives in which history is commonly presented. (Because I taught history for nearly 10 years, in public secondary education and in higher education, and because I have multiple degrees in history, I know this is unfortunately still the case.) To deviate from those ways of viewing the past, which promote an imbalanced perspective, each particular Moraga will be observed through a different historical lens. I hope this will give you a deeper and more realistic understanding of the Mexican-American's past and experiences. Exploring each significant Moraga through these lenses in turn will provide an elegant backdrop while we examine their lives. Outside of the conventional narrative, the "Pilgrims and Plymouth Rock" interpretation, we can see a different history, which shines with its own light.

Chapter 2
The Moor Expulsion

Spain in the Medieval Period

TO CONTEXTUALIZE THE MORAGAS in their respective eras, we need to examine the world stage both *before* and *during* the times they lived in. I found one of the earliest recorded Moraga names during the medieval period, on the peripheries of an important event in Spanish history. In the thirteenth century, a man named Arias Moragas watched as the first steps were taken to reclaim the Iberian Peninsula in the name of Catholicism. But, we need to understand when and where he lived to understand him.

Pre-Medieval and Medieval Spain

LIKE VIRTUALLY ALL OF THE COUNTRIES in the world, Spain is in a constant state of "cultural" flux and has been evolving since humans settled in the region thousands of years ago. Spain, as we know it today, really did not form until about five centuries ago. Before the 1500s, the Iberian Peninsula was comprised of various kingdoms with their own cultures and languages. Throughout history, these kingdoms traded with and warred against one another. Large kingdoms acquired others and grew larger, while smaller ones disappeared entirely. Even Spain today is by no means a culturally unified country – the Basques of northern Spain and the Catalonians in the East, among others, have their own distinct cultures and languages, which are significantly different from the rest of the country.

But in Arias Moragas's time, and long before, those cultural differences had political borders.

In the Classical period, the Greeks first referred to the

peninsula as "Iberia" named after the river Iberos. Mediterranean traders utilized it for its ports. In the second century BCE, the Romans created a permanent settlement there and referred to it by its Punic name "Hispanae." Later, they would introduce Christianity and establish major cities, such as Barcelona, Pamplona and Cordoba. Barcelona was originally a Roman military camp (also known as "Faventia"), while Pamplona was named after the great Roman leader Pompeii (same as the infamous lost city), and Cordoba was named after the Numidian leader who first conquered the city. As the Western Roman Empire began to fall around the fifth century CE, the German Visigothic dynasties took control of the region. Long periods of political, economic and social instability followed.

By the eighth century, the Ummayad Caliphate[2] brought Islam to the Middle East, Persia, North Africa, *and* into what we know as today as Spain. Under Tariq Ibn Zayid, a band of Northern Africans Islamic Berbers (also called "Moors") capitalized on that period of Visigoth instability, invading the Iberian Peninsula in 711. By 732, they firmly occupied much of the region and had penetrated beyond the Pyrenees Mountains, close to present day France. Their march into Europe was stopped by Charles Martel at the Battle of Tours, but outside of the complete conquest of the Basque and Asturian areas, most of the Iberian Peninsula came under Moor control by the mid eighth century.

For the next 750 years, the Moors held a firm presence in the region, but power over specific areas vacillated constantly between Christian and Islamic hands. When seen through a contemporary perspective, you might imagine that Christian and Muslim administrations would struggle to rule over each other's peoples, but this was not necessarily the case. Many Christians came to accept their Muslim leaders and lived contentedly under their rule, while many Muslims embraced Christian leaders.[3] These same allegiances applied to the region's militaries too. Many times, the so-called "Christian armies" (which were not standing armies as we know them today) were made up of mercenary groups that included Christians, Jews *and* Muslims. Many Moor armies were composed of the same mix of religious and ethnic groups fighting alongside each other.[4] By the late 9th century, Al-Andalus – what the Moors called their Spain – became the jewel of Muslim power. They made their capital in Cordoba, one of the most advanced intellectual hubs of the world. Interestingly enough, although the Abbasid dynasty eventually ousted the Umayyad caliphate from most of the Islamic empire, Al-Andalus remained under Umayyad rule. In a sense, ironically, Al-Andalus in Europe became the first independent state in the Islamic empire.

It was also during the 800s that some of the first Islamic regions would fall back into Christian hands. Soon after the Moors established themselves, the Counts of Barcelona (Catalonian royalty from the northeastern region of Al-Andulus) banded with Visigoth nobles from present-day France, who had retained some of their power after the Moor conquests. From then on, the Catalonians continued to be the proverbial thorn in the side of the Moorish kingdoms, because from their center of power in the north, the Spanish "Reconquista"[5] would slowly work its way south. Yet though easy to classify this Christian reconquest as a struggle for religious power over Al-Andalus, reality was much more complex. Details of this era often gloss over the fact that the North African Almohad dynasty had found its way into prospering Al-Andalus in the early second millennium, and a strict treatment of the native Moor populations swayed opinions of their new leadership, resulting in discontent. Though religion did play a significant role in the eventual outcome of these lands, it would be better to view this era as more of a civil war that just happened to include religious conquest. It was not solely about whose church, temple or mosque the people wanted to attend.

Unhappy citizens sometimes side with the advancing armies instead of the unpopular rulers making the people miserable at home, and that was true during this time as well.

In addition to this, by the second millennium, Islamic territories in the Middle East were growing stronger than the Catholic church, which sent it on a radical trajectory within Europe. Christian forces—under papal decree of Urban II—were first sent to recapture the holy city of Jerusalem and to establish Crusader states in present day Syria, Palestine, Israel and Lebanon. Again, though religion played a major role within the Crusades, economic and territorial expansion were just as important.

Religion aside, a lot of the world's wealth at the time was concentrated in the Middle East, and "protecting one's faith" may have been a strategic guise to gain support for a war of expansion into the eastern Muslim world during a time when most of Western Europe suffered economically.

Pope Urban II set a precedent that would further develop under Pope Innocent III in the twelfth and thirteenth centuries, going from framing attacks as a foreign campaign, to a promise to rid Western Europe of heresy. A simple war the people couldn't afford...but a Catholic crusade that they would pay for.

This play on the fervent stance of belief was not really a surprise because the "Great Schism" had only a few centuries earlier divided the European Catholic church with the Greek Orthodox Church. Further division within W. Europe would continue to destabilize the church limiting papal influence throughout the region. Pope Innocent III capitalized on the anti-Islamic rhetoric and momentum gathered by the Crusades in the Middle East to launch his own war within Europe itself.

Arias Moragas and the Battle of Las Navas de Tolosa

BY THE THIRTEENTH CENTURY, soldiers from the Catholic kingdoms in southeastern France, who were known as the Ultramontanos[6], along with armies from the Iberian kingdoms of Portugal, Leon, Castile, Aragon, and Navarre, worked together to expel the Moors from these lands. Prior to this, the kingdoms had either been focused on dealing with internal turmoil or on struggling against each other. With the coming of the Almohad caliphate, things had changed. "Miramamolin" Al Nasir, the Almohad Caliph of Al-Andalus, began to reclaim disputed Moorish lands in the Salvatierra region of Castile by the early thirteenth century. Under Alphonso VIII of Castile, international funding and the ecclesiastical support of Pope Innocent III supported an effort to "reclaim" these lands again by pushing the Moors southward. The eventual "tipping" of lands formerly under Moorish control, putting them into the hands of the Catholic Church and the kings of the Iberian Peninsula, culminated in the Battle of Las Navas de Tolosa in 1212. This was the final straw, ultimately confining the Moors to Granada in southern Spain until their complete expulsion during the Reconquista in 1492.

Arias Moragas, the first Moraga we're going to examine, was probably a lesser Catalonian knight[7] from the county of Barcelona. He would have ridden for the king of Aragon, Pedro II, who was documented for playing a significant role in the battle.

As a Catalonian, Arias came from an area that prided itself on being a hotbed of Moor resistance since it was directly to the south of the kingdoms that were able to resist conquest and was the first kingdom to successfully retake Christian lands back from the Moors. Moreover, Barcelona was a key port to the Holy Land during the Crusades, and the Christian fervency brought back by pilgrims through this port added to the already intense Catholic attitudes there. Lastly, Catalonia was set up as a feudal society, more like the rest of Western Europe than its neighbors to its south. The shared values this feudalism promoted with its neighbors to the north only added to their resistance to the Moor rule.

We know that Arias Moragas was a knight but not one of nobility. This means that he might not have inherited his title from his family, but Arias easily could have been a lesser knight or a soldier who was knighted after the battle. Knighthood—and what allowed one to become a knight—was changing during the twelfth and thirteenth centuries in Spain. Aside from being immensely pious, one needed to own a warhorse, a very costly animal at the time. This implies that Arias was either wealthy enough to buy one, he was popular enough to be given one, or he had claimed one from a vanquished enemy after the battle. (Archbishop Jimenez de Rada mentions the Aragon contingent helping itself to loot after the fight.[8]) Arias's equipment likely was similar to other knights; we can guess that he wore a mix of chain mail and plated armor, and he must have known how to fight with a lance while mounted on his horse, because that was another requisite for knighthood during the period. Each of his weapons and pieces of major equipment would have had religious or chivalrous significance, based on what we know about other knights of the same period. Ramon Llul, who wrote about Knighthood in Catalonia in the thirteenth century, describes one such weapon, "Unto the knight is given a sword which is made in the shape of a cross to signify that as just as our lord Jesus Christ vanquished on the Cross the death into which we had fallen because of the sin of our father Adam, so the knight must vanquish and destroy the enemies of the Cross with the sword."[9]

Prior to the actual fighting at Las Navas De Tolosa, the Pedro II contingent helped overtake the Fort of Malagon, which had fallen into the hands of the Moor forces under Miramamolin. The day before they arrived, a French contingent was able to storm and force the inhabitants to surrender. When Arias and the other soldiers arrived, they became more involved in looting the fortress than in any sort of battle. The surrender negotiated by Pedro II at first called for the destruction of the fort. Catholic clergymen who had once occupied it begged them to leave it standing, which they were granted, but again Pedro's men claimed half of its contents while the other half was left for the Nevarran contingents.

On July 6, 1212, the fighting began at Las Navas de Tolosa. The lord of Vizcaya of Navarre commanded the troops at the front of the collected armies, Pedro II of Aragon commanded the left flank (which included Arias), and Sancho of Navarre led the troops on the right. Alfonso VIII commanded the middle section, while the Ultramontanos and other religious military orders[10] were at the rear. This massive Christian army invaded Miramamolin's army encampment at Santa Elena (in the Jaen region of present day Granada, Spain), and during the first stages of the battle, the encampment lines were broken. Although the Viscay contingent were the first to enter the battle, the left and the right flanks of the battle lines held fast while Alfonso VIII himself entered into the melee and made his way to Miramamolin's tent, breaking through the human chain of slaves that guarded the caliph. Though Miramamolin escaped, fleeing to Baeza, he was eventually found and killed.

Arias witnessed and participated in both an actual crusade *and* a battle that led to a major shift in power in the Iberian Peninsula—one that has left an indelible mark on Spanish society. He is our first Moraga, our introduction to a time that would continue to play a role in Spain and world history up until today. But though the Castilian and Aragonese kingdoms forced the Moors into the south, this did not mean *all* of the Moors left. Our next chapter will focus on two Moragas living as "Moriscos" under Catholic rule during the Spanish Inquisition.

Chapter 3
The Inquisition and the "Moriscos"

FOR THE NEXT TWO HUNDRED YEARS, Catholic kingdoms throughout Spain consolidated their power. After the Battle of Las Navas de Tolosa, the Moor kingdoms were slowly driven into present-day Grenada. Castile and Aragon eventually absorbed several of the smaller Christian kingdoms nearby. As power shifted further into Christian hands in Western Europe, and with the new Ottoman rule in the east, the Islamic empires of Africa began to decline, so they could do nothing as the main kingdoms that would soon unify to become Spain materialized.

Christianity would continue to be used as a political tool but this time to bolster unification in its reconquered lands on the Iberian Peninsula. Within these years we will explore the lives of Jeronimo and Antonio Moraga. Like Arias Moragas' story, their roles in history are more clearly understood if one examines their historical circumstances. Jeronimo and Antonio's stories are particularly distinct because of their "Morisco," or Moor ancestry.

Spanish Unification

AS CHRISTIAN KINGDOMS RECONCILED and consolidated through the fifteenth and sixteenth centuries, they grew in a slow but painstaking process, with the Catholic Church's help (ignited by Innocent III's crusader influence in Castile and Aragon) and the momentum they had gathered through the reclamation of the Iberian Peninsula. The civic and royal authorities of both Castile and Aragon pressed firmly for inter-kingdom consolidation, mainly in their regions, first in areas they could easily control, then throughout the peninsula as they gained a foothold against the

Moor kingdoms of the south. Yet, years of constant infighting between smaller kingdoms and larger ones under a weak Iberian feudal system plagued the land during the process. Contract mercenary groups were a constant problem. These mercenaries were often led by "Hidalgos" (another word for "robber barons") who claimed unofficial rule over any lands in which they fought. Reacting to this, "cortes" (courts) were set up throughout the countryside, and by the late 1400s both Queen Isabella of Castile and the Aragonese royalty ascended their thrones as a solid effort was already underway to quell the hidalgo issue.

When Ferdinand gained the monarchy of Aragon and wed Queen Isabella of Castile in 1469, they inherited a fragile yet slowly stabilizing society. Through their efforts, Spain would come closer to resembling a single unified kingdom. By 1492, both Aragon and Castile had completely enveloped the smaller kingdoms surrounding them, and together, their king and queen effectively ruled Spain. The Catholic monarchs[11] also completed the "Reconquista" by expelling the last of the Moor kings into North Africa. After they did this, they adopted policies that eventually mandated all remaining Jews and Moors either leave or convert to Catholicism. It was an attempt to further unify the region, but it also helped the Church garner more influence and momentum in the Iberian Peninsula by gaining new converts. This would also help circumvent the threats the Protestant movement and the Ottomans presented to the church at the time.

Nonetheless, Iberia's non-Christian communities had centuries-old roots throughout the region and considerable influence, which exacerbated unity and control issues for Isabella and Ferdinand. Newly converted Muslims and Jews post-Reconquista converted because it was compulsory, but for many, it was only a public declaration and did not necessarily reflect a change in either their personal religious or social behavior. The early years of forced Catholicism seem to be have been coupled with a lax approach both by the crown and the church, but tolerance disintegrated as Castile-Aragon unification strengthened.

To clampdown on any potential subversion, civil seizure of land fractured the formerly Jewish and Islamic communities causing a strategic relocation that contributed to their further collapse. As the crown appropriated land, Spanish Jews (now called "Conversos") moved to more Jewish-friendly regions while Moors ("Moriscos") would often move to areas of economic opportunity. Though Moriscos did not necessarily compose the upper socio-economic levels at this time for obvious reasons, by the time of the Reconquista and for some time after they were known for trade knowledge and skilled labor.

Ecclesiastical authority also would play a major role in religious unification as well by pushing and forcing conversion through the use of tribunals known as the "Inquisition." Despite what is commonly written about the events in the typical histories of the Spanish Inquisition, it was much more complex than merely the systematic trial and execution of Jews in Spain—although this was one of the many terrors associated with it.

Though its roles evolved during its existence, the Inquisition was, for brevity's sake, an ecclesiastical system of committees with a goal of fostering religious and political unity throughout Spain. It was a type of secret police that enforced Catholic traditions, rules and customs and punished heresy, which for the most part was anything that refuted Catholicism or anything that threatened to undermine the new state. Torture and execution of Jews, Muslims and eventually Protestants was widely implemented, but technically extermination was not its goal.

The Church didn't call for a mass killing like it had during the first Crusades in the Middle East, when it had been deemed permissible to take a Saracen's (Muslim) life. Because religious minorities played such a large and integral part of proto-Spanish society, their populations could not be eliminated; it would have been detrimental to the delicate economic infrastructures of the new monarchy. When the Catholic monarchs reigned, many of the targeted Jews and Moriscos were considerably wealthier and more influential than their Catholic neighbors. So, religion aside, the aim of the Inquisition was to subdue any potential threat to the fragile kingdom of budding Spain, fiscally support the presence of the church in Spain, and later, to *preserve* Spain's new unity.

By the rise of the absolute monarch Charles V, along with the Catholic-Counter reformation in the 1500s and the colonization of regions in the "New World,"[12] vast resources were made available to the Inquisition as a tool to bolster the crown's growing power. Torture and execution began to play more of a significant role in trials, as it became relentless in enforcing both religious and political unity. Inquisition affairs and trials started to overlap with local affairs.[13] The bureaucracy of the Inquisition eventually became shrouded in secrecy, and the capricious methods by which tribunals deemed "heresy" (along with treatment of prisoners) contributed to widespread paranoia… especially among non-Catholics. Nevertheless, the Inquisition still worked to seize wealth by exacting fees and appropriating land, in addition to using non-lethal forms of punishment to solidify unity. For example, the Moriscos under Hapsburg dynastic rule in the sixteenth and seventeenth centuries often found the sentence of rowing for the imperial navy was the punishment set aside especially for them.

It is under these circumstances in the late 1500s that the Inquisition experiences of two Moragas, Jeronimo and Antonio, took place.

Abduction and Secrecy

MANY MORISCOS HAD CONVERTED to Christianity, but since they were the descendants of Moors or Moor converts, their behavior and movements were carefully scrutinized by their municipalities and by the Inquisition. The case of Jeronimo Moraga, a descendant of Morisco Christian converts (and therefore still considered a Morisco) shows all too well the uncertainty and unpredictability Moriscos often felt during the Inquisition years commonly referred to as the "Great Fear."

Jeronimo Moraga was called to stand trial before the Inquisition in 1577 for the general charge of "conspiracy." This charge was not rare in Aragon during this time because it was used for a variety of smaller offenses. He lived in Zaragoza, a Morisco bastion, which had been the old city fortress of Al-Jafaria prior to the Reconquista, and which hosted more than 900 inquisition trials during 1568–1620.[14] For Jeronimo, the Inquisition was a major part of life. Under its watchful eye, he had to monitor his actions carefully because Inquisition collaborators throughout Zaragosa were plentiful. Prisoners were often forced or coerced to spy on

Moraga Deconstructed

neighbors and citizens. His was a time of uneasy peace and bloody revolt. He knew the punishments inflicted on his community, he'd witnessed his neighbors' maltreatment by the Inquisition, and he would have known about the disappearances.

Matthew Carr states in his book *Blood and Faith*, "...The Aragon Inquisition prosecuted a higher percentage of Moor descendants than in any other part of the country, sending so many to galley slavery that Philip II recommended in 1560 that the same punishment be extended to Moriscos elsewhere in Spain."[15] King Phillip II expanded Morisco persecution because he wanted to show his power—not only to the strong Morisco communities but also to other populations of Aragon who were still expressing resentment at coming under control of the kingdom of Castile.

Jeronimo's case is particularly intriguing because he was charged not just with conspiracy but more specifically, "speaking to those who had taken an oath of secrecy." His offense: He inquired about his father and brother who had been missing for a year.

Abduction was a common tactic used by the Inquisition to scare people into confessing or at least looking the other way when arrests were made. Since his family members had disappeared, and he hadn't heard anything in so long, Jeronimo believed the Inquisition had arrested them. To verify this, he spoke to people the Inquisition had previously put on trial, which was illegal.

On his way to an *Auto de Fe* (admittance of heresy and/or guilt in front of church officials and public), Jeronimo spoke to two men who had already sworn to the Inquisition not to talk about any prisoners that might still be held. Jeronimo knew they weren't allowed to tell him but asked anyway.[16] By inquiring, the two men could claim Jeronimo was acting "conspiratorially"; he was arrested, sentenced and fined.

Burned at the Stake

IN THE TOWN OF ARCOS DE LA MEDINACELI, in the Cuenca region of Spain in Castile, Antonio Moraga, a town leader, was asked by the Inquisitorial commissioner Dr. Aranda to gather Moriscos for a list of "non-Christian" transgressions.[17] Antonio agreed. During the following year, a number of Moriscos came forth and confessed to these transgressions, including Beatriz Padilla, with whom Antonio would eventually develop an intimate relationship. These confessions proved to the Inquisition that Arcos de la Medinaceli was a "hotbed" of Morisco activity, and they decided that close observation of the town's inhabitants was required. In 1581, the Inquisition sent Marcos Fernando De Almanza—reportedly, a drunk and lecherous priest[18]—to oversee the town. De Almanza "accused Antonio of having celebrated the defeat of the Portuguese king Sebastian in Morocco with a bullfight, inciting local Moriscos not to pay tithes to the Church, and calling his children 'little Moors.'"[19] By then, Antonio was living (unmarried) with Beatriz Padilla, something that was not completely unheard of in Renaissance Western Europe but not condoned by the church. Because of De Almanza, the Inquisition imprisoned Antonio for "conspiracy" for two years. Given his behavior afterward, Almanza might have accused Antonio in an effort to gain sexual access to Beatriz Padilla or may have suggested heavier sentencing to punish the couple for living together out of wedlock. Even after Antonio's release, the Inquisition continued to persecute Beatriz Padilla, who bore Antonio Moraga's son while in prison. Sadly, the Inquisition later tortured Beatriz and burned her at the stake on false conspiracy charges. Very likely she was executed because she refused to accept Almanza's advances, but it didn't help her case that she and Antonio had children out of wedlock. Obviously, like any other institution in Europe at the time, corruption took many forms in the Inquisition.

Under King Phillip II, Spain's economy consistently faltered, continuing through the late sixteenth and seventeenth centuries. Though the Morisco Moragas stayed put, determined to live through the particularly turbulent times in Spain, many other Spanish had already begun to seek their fortunes across the ocean.

During the early sixteenth century, the first North American Moragas arrived in the Caribbean.

Chapter 4
The Caribbean Natives

DURING THE INQUISITION and the concurrent unification of Spain, the Spanish explored the North and South American continents and would eventually conquer then pacify their indigenous populations. The resources and opportunities these new lands offered attracted many Europeans. Under the Hapsburg dynasty, Spain would come to rule the most powerful empire in Europe with colonies throughout the world. The European exploration of North and South America, the establishment of the Treaty of Tordesillas in 1494,[20] and the pressure from the Catholic Counter-Reformation to convert new Catholics prompted the Spanish to construct a sophisticated international trading and mission network that allowed the empire to expand both commercially and religiously. We don't know why the first Moragas immigrated to the New World, but we have clear records that they did so during the 1500s. Some would eventually settle in present-day Chile; this branch of the Moragas likely came from the city Caceres in the Extremadura region in central Spain where there is a "Casa de Moragas," which is currently a craft shop, in the medieval section of the city. The Moragas that settled in the Caribbean and into Mexico left Spain under a cloud of mystery, but once they landed in the New World, they found colonies fraught with conflict between the self-interested Spanish military, the Catholic Church, businessmen seeking to expand their profits, Caribbean natives, slaves...and settlers.

Martin De Moraga and Native Resistance in Caribbean
MARTIN DE MORAGA WAS FROM BAEZA, SPAIN, and ship manifests

indicate he immigrated to Cuba in 1512.[21] Though not much is known about Martin, the fact that he was among the first generations of Spanish settlers in the New World deserves mention. Typical narratives about this point in history convey conquistador successes but rarely expand on their shortcomings or look deeply at the formidable resistance organized by indigenous natives. Martin De Moraga was in Cuba when the Spanish were in the primary stages of colonizing, so he would have been able to see them actively pacifying native populations and establishing agricultural settlements. He would have likely seen the initial failures as well. The Spanish used the same brutal method of colonization in the Caribbean that they used in the Canary Islands off the African coast,[22] and Cuba was the third major island in the Caribbean conquered by the Spanish, after Hispanola[23] and Puerto Rico.

Though the *Nina*, the *Pinta*, and the *Santa Maria* had stumbled onto the Americas, their monetary goal remained the focus of the voyage, even if they had missed their target in Asia entirely. So early Spanish exploration in the Caribbean had largely been business ventures and not necessarily for wider exploration although Columbus' voyages are still often touted as those of discovery and wonder in the typical narrative. After that initial pacification and settlement, Europeans introduced different methods of agriculture into the Caribbean, hoping to produce resource commodities. They also began to look for gold. They did both by first setting up semi-friendly relations with the native "Aruaco" people (who Europeans would later refer to as "Tainos" and "Caribe" populations) but eventually, those relationships ended in atrocities. This included some exportation of the indigenous population as slaves to Europe and other parts of the Americas, enslavement in the Caribbean, and by the late sixteenth century, the near decimation of the natives from disease and forced labor condoned by the crown through what is referred to as "Encomienda."

In 1511, the Tainos were already being enslaved as workers forced to search for gold and as menial labor for building and agricultural production throughout the Caribbean. The islands offered the climate necessary to produce one of the most desired commodities of the time – sugar. When it became clearer that the Spanish were aggressively expanding throughout the islands, natives moved themselves away from the settlers, making new homes in less-desired areas. As they realized they were dying, not only through forced enslavement but also from disease because of European contact, many isolated themselves further. When there was nowhere left to run, many resorted to suicide by hanging themselves, poisoning, and jumping from cliffs.[24]

Despite the fact that it is often written that the Spanish saw natives as somewhat docile,[25] many tribes *violently* resisted Spanish occupation. Some led organized revolts, and by 1511 there were serious uprisings occurring throughout Cuba. Martin De Moraga was in Cuba in 1512 as a new European settler on the island, he probably lived in the newly established settlement of "Barracoa" or near it and witnessed the severe pacification and maltreatment of natives. Conflict between the Spanish and the natives was a routine occurrence; active settlement had only begun one year prior to Martin landing in Cuba, and the Spanish didn't complete the cities of Havana and Santiago until some years later after that. Because of the discovery of the southern coast of the North American continent, by 1512 the city of Baracoa (in addition to being an agricultural venture) was being utilized as a supply port for ships going to the North American mainland. Martin would have walked among the immense jungles and greenery of native Cuba and undoubtedly helped with Spanish expansion throughout it. His governor was Diego Velazques de Cuellar, who was known for conquering Cuba as well as aggressively helping to pacify the natives throughout the Caribbean and Mayan Mexico. Velazques was also known for his particularly violent methods, which likely added to the Caribbean's colonization issues.

Martin De Moraga would have been familiar with the term "Cacique," which meant "native chief" in the Taino language, and because of the particular time period that he was on the island, had to have been aware of both the mass suicides and the native resistance led by "Hatuey," a Cacique from the island of Hispanola.

Hatuey was famous for being one of the first markedly successful Taino freedom fighters in the Caribbean and among the first to collaborate with African slaves in a combined multinational resistance effort.[26] After mounting opposition in response to Velazquez's treatment of the natives in Hispanola, he organized in Cuba in 1511 where the rebellion had reached its height. The Spanish ultimately captured Hatuey in Cuba and burned him at the stake on February 2, 1512. Given that Martin De Moraga was in Cuba at that time, he would have been among the first people in the world to hear of Hatuey's death speech (made famous by early native rights proponent Bartolome de Las Casas[27]) in which Hatuey concludes, "If there are Spaniards in heaven, then I would rather burn in Hell…" Martin's life in the early Spanish Caribbean was likely harsh, difficult and fraught with incredible turmoil. Yet this experience would have been different from those Spanish that ventured onto mainland North and South America in later years.

Chapter 5
The Mainland

THE COLONIZATION METHODS used in the conquest of the Caribbean proved disastrous for the Spanish in terms of sustainability. Though they eventually quelled the native resistance and began resource production for exportation, the atmosphere the Europeans had created in the Caribbean was one of blistering violence, death and staggering maltreatment of the natives. For all intents and purposes, because it was so slow to set up resource production along with the demise of the indigenous peoples, early colonization in the Caribbean was considered a failure.

As attitudes shifted in Europe and the Catholic Counter-Reformation was launched as a reaction to the Protestant Reformation in the fifteenth and sixteenth centuries, the Catholic Church adopted new policies that did not wholly condone native slavery. Famous enlightened thinkers like the aforementioned Las Casas influenced new religious policy, which emphasized better native treatment. Of course, the Spanish continued to expand, colonize, and murder in the New World for a long time after this shift began and despite this newfound morality geared towards natives, it was not offered to African slaves that were imported to the Americas. Yet despite these obvious shortcomings, the church also saw these native populations as new conversion opportunities, and it followed that new religiously condoned methods of pacification were adopted in what was now the fully functioning colony of New Spain.

North American Conquest

HERNAN CORTEZ OF MEDELLIN, SPAIN, understood the Spanish would not conquer the powerful Mexica (or Aztec) empire in present day Mexico in the same way the Spanish before him had conquered the Caribbean. The indigenous populations were too large, and Mexico's lands were too vast. Cortez's approach would need to rely more heavily upon promoting friction between different Mexica tribes and taking advantage of this instability to control the elite. We know that the Spanish in the Americas would eventually come to rely on Cortez's methods because they were thoroughly documented. Other conquistadors who had goals in the New World—like Francisco Pizarro, the conqueror of the Inca Empire in South America—would use his methods as well.

After consolidating power, the church introduced a new conversion system to the New World in lieu of Encomienda: now, priests essentially exchanged conversion and labor for housing and food within Catholic missions. Their construction was often left to native converts, and eventually priests educated them within their halls. Cities, towns and "pueblos" would often grow out of the missions. Though this new system of conversion did not prevent the atrocities of colonization from occurring, they were not as horrific as those in the Caribbean.

Military conquest on the mainland evolved differently as well. Conquistadors who went to North and South American only conquered the strongest tribes, and not necessarily all of them. For generations after the initial takeovers, the Spanish would have to continually quell uprisings and insurrections while at the same time forming diplomatic and trade relationships with the indigenous populations.

The Yaqi and the Mayo Natives

PABLO DE MORAGA was born in the Sonora region of Northern Mexico in 1604 nearly one hundred years after Martin De Moraga settled in Cuba, and his ancestry is said to be of Basque origins. At this time in New Spain, the Spanish were still actively expanding throughout present-day northern Mexico and into the southwestern region of what is now the United States. Although the Spanish military initially conquered and subjugated the natives in northwestern Mexico,[28] the church was now growing into this region as well and instituting ecclesiastical policies that aided in the colonization processes. By 1604, when Pablo was born, the Spanish had only settled in the areas of present-day Sinaloa, the region to the south of Sonora. He likely lived in a frontier territory in the southern region of present-day Sonora during the pacification of the Yaqi and Mayo Native American tribes that inhabited this mountainous arid region. But because he was born outside of Sinaloa, which was outside of the protection of the military, he likely came from humbler means.

Around the time Pablo was four, the Spanish forced the Mayo people to enter into a diplomatic relationship with the Yaqi, and two years later, the Spanish took over with aid from the Mayo. We can compare Martin De Moraga's life during the era of the resistance fighter Hatuey and the suppression of the Tainos in the Caribbean with Pablo's experience with the Yaqi and Mayo. Though initially similar, Pablo's life would have been different from Martin's as the years progressed. If Pablo stayed in Sinaloa/Sonora his entire life, he would have seen the slow, at times painful, assimilation of the Yaqui and the Mayo into the New Spanish society throughout his life and would have frequently interacted with them as well. He would have observed their religious conversion and them being absorbed into New Spanish society seeing many become laborers and ranch workers. Because these tribes relied on the specific agricultural knowledge needed to work these arid lands, the Spanish utilized natives to work on the ranches and haciendas. Conversely, Martin De Moraga would have seen the ruthless oppression of the Caribbean natives and their forced labor. He would have lived in constant fear of being attacked. This is not so much the case with Pablo.

Pablo likely walked the dry dusty roads of early Sonora among its new ranches as an adult in drab loose clothing, wide-brimmed hat, high boots, and probably carried a harquebus – an early rifle – and bladed weapons to protect himself. He would have lived in an adobe building, and his life would have been considerably influenced by the Jesuit order that had started to construct missions throughout the region. Because he lived in an area of budding agriculture, especially cattle ranching, he was either a ranch hand or farmer. Many of the techniques he learned for ranching would have come from the native populations, but he would have also used European methods as well.

Having been from Sonora, Pablo had to have known about Captain Pedro de Perea who ventured into the Sonoran interior to claim the territory for the crown and exploit its rich mineral resources and farmland. He likely visited the first missions in the regions and the Spanish forts known as "presidios," since these were centers of commerce, colonial European culture, and local trade. Disease and strife did come as a result of Spanish colonization in this region and there was tension – Yaqi uprisings occurred up until the twentieth century, but there was a difference between native interactions on the mainland than those of the Caribbean. Unlike the almost-complete decimation of the Aruaco in Cuba, there were still close to 20,000 Yaquis and 10,000–15,000 Mayos[29] concentrated in parts of the Sonora region in the seventeenth century, and they did not isolate themselves from the Spanish invaders. Again, Pablo lived in a time when there was close contact with these indigenous populations and he lived among them.

During Pablo Moraga's lifetime, the Spanish had been in the New World for more than a century, and there were different social dynamics set into motion by the integration of European laws and social norms into the New World. Though they were gradually introduced and, on the surface, might appear to be nonthreatening, their eventual effects were significant in establishing control of the colonies. The next section will examine Rosa Texarra Moraga and her place in this vastly changing New Spanish society.

Chapter 6
Diversity, Marriage, and Property in Early Eighteenth Century New Spain

Gender and Diversity in New Spain

THE TOPIC OF GENDER in Colonial Latin America is still thoroughly understated in modern history and rarely touched upon even though some of the earliest New World feminist thought on gender was written by Juana Inez de la Cruz of New Spain in the seventeenth century. The complexities of the social interactions developing between Europeans, Africans, and the indigenous populations during this time are compelling on many levels yet the Western European patriarchal dominance of history still has yet to shed as much light on this topic as it should. In the case of New Spanish Mexico, the church played a critical role in introducing concepts and enforcing mores regarding gender, diversity, and marriage, which though social in nature also had very real economic motivations as well.

Africans, particularly those from West Africa, played a very important role in Latin American history, but their experience, like those of the indigenous populations, essentially was erased. Much of this has to do with the fact that when natives and African slaves were converted, Spanish names were conferred upon them, thereby starting a Euro-lineage and in most cases doing away with native ones. Outside of lineage, titles including "Criollo," "Peninsulares," and "Mestizo" became common during the eighteenth century as reflections of social status and cultural mixes which promoted racial divisions with echoes that are still very apparent today in

Latin American countries. Yet the most fundamental factor that remains in determining status in the New World, more so than race, was gender. It is within these years of early modern colonial social subtleties, patriarchy, and changing gender dynamics, we will examine our first Moraga female.

Rosa Texarra Moraga

ROSA TEXARRA MORAGA was born in 1710. She married into the Moraga family by wedding Juan Joseph Moraga,[30] a soldier who would later be stationed on the frontier in present-day Tucson, Arizona, at the Tubac Presidio in the Pimeria Alta region of Colonial Spain. Although it is said Rosa's family was from the Altar region of Sonora in Mexico, the city had not been established until some sixty years after she was born. She was probably from the northern frontiers of Sinaloa/Sonora close to Altar and the Spanish frontier, which was moving steadily north during her lifetime. She also lived in a particularly dangerous environment: During the first half of the eighteenth century, Pima and Apaches – natives in the northern areas of present-day Mexico – consistently attacked the Spanish frontier in Sonora.

Rosa would have walked among bustling cattle ranches of Sonora and among fields of grain that would have been planted in the way that was introduced by the Spanish some twenty years before. Given the lack of a strong centralized government in the area, church leaders would have functioned as her civic leaders, and the Jesuit missions and churches near her would have been the social centers of her life outside of the home. In her teens she, like Pablo Moraga, witnessed a boom in silver, and the mining industry becoming an even stronger institution in her region.

In colonial Spain during the eighteenth century, women, depending on wealth and status, had few official options in life – generally only marriage, or becoming a nun. However, despite the rampant patriarchy that pervaded the New Spanish society in which she lived, Rosa (like other Spanish colonial women in the eighteenth century) was able to own and could inherit land.[31] This aside, the Spanish brought the European marriage social mechanism to the New World and began to heavily promote it within native communities which looked upon women and men as parallel or complimentary sources of authority.[32] Susan Kellog noted in her book, *Law and the Transformation of Aztec Culture*, that, "The Early Catholic priests hoped to use Christian marriages of high elites and their children of marriageable age as examples for the indigenous natives."[33] As natives, slaves, and Europeans commingled and as the Spanish presence became stronger, non-Euro ideas of gender dissipated. New Spanish society in turn pressed European gender models of male superiority and wives as property. Outside of changing gender norms, there were also considerable legal reasons for promoting and enforcing the idea of Christian marriage to natives. Spanish society and lawmakers hoped conjugal monogamous unions would influence natives to indirectly embrace European colonial probate and kin-based inheritance laws.

Obviously this issue had been a source of friction within New Spanish society because indigenous families were often polygamous, with higher-ranking men on the social ladder having as many as a hundred wives.[34] Kin-based family units could theoretically hand over property and other goods both horizontally and vertically to both men and women.[35] During Rosa's time, the colonial governments and churches had to function more autonomously without the help of the crown, which was increasingly occupied with issues in Europe. Therefore, New Spain needed to capitalize on as many resources as it could, so it developed legal avenues for seizing property through wills and inheritance laws limiting how property could be passed along. Monogamous Christian marriage promoted the passing of property only to offspring of married couples and legally allowed local governments and the church to seize property in many situations. So the Spanish continued to push the idea of the nuclear family and New World European marriages (like Rosa's) in order to establish a firmer legal grip on inheritance and probate among natives thereby asserting more control within the colonies. In much the same way that the crown at one time had legally endorsed forced native subjugation under the Encomienda system, European, Christian, marriages became yet another channel in which the Spanish would continue to colonize and subjugate its conquered peoples.

Chapter 7
Eighteenth Century New Spanish Frontiers

AS COLONIAL SPANISH HISTORY UNFOLDED, different international agendas were on separate trajectories across the American continents. In the late 1700s, the west coast of today's continental United States was still a possession of Spain. In fact, the Spanish claimed more than a third of what is now considered the continental United States after the French ceded lands to them in 1762 in the Treaty of Foutainebleau. The U.S. would then go on to claim much of these remaining Louisiana lands in North America by 1803 through the Louisiana Purchase. Interestingly enough, the birth of the United States in 1776 coincided with Spanish exploration and settlement of the North American west and southwest. Tucson, San Diego and San Francisco already had been founded by that same year.

To be clear, these were not cities the British colonists or Americans established but had been there long before, although Americans helped make them flourish after they acquired those areas following the Mexican-American War.[36]

In 1776, the Spanish settled cities along the present-day California coast and in Arizona, but with an insufficient Spanish presence in these regions, international interests brought explorers and hunters to the shorelines of California and the American Northwest, known at the time as the Alta California region of New Spain. By this time, the British and later the Americans were sending parties in attempts to lay unofficial claim to these unsettled territories.[37] Even more serious was the issue of the early Russian American Company (RAC) continually working its way along the west coast of North America throughout the 1700s. Through the marriage of Nikolai Rezenov of the RAC to the Spanish-born Concepcion Arguello, the Russian American Company was able to gain access to the northern California coasts and allowed to hunt sea otter pelts. By 1812, it even established a small settlement in present-day Sonoma County, California, naming it Fort Ross.

Because of these forays into Spanish territory, the crown mandated an increased Spanish presence in these areas and called for their exploration, mapping and the pacification of natives, along with the founding of settlements and Catholic missions. This would ensure that any settlement by non-Spanish Europeans would not go unchecked. It is during these expeditions and the Spanish settlement of the North American west and southwest that the next Moragas will be examined.

Jose Joaquin Moraga

JOSE JOAQUIN MORAGA was probably born in the Altar region of Sonora, and luckily, Catholic church documents and military records paint a relatively accurate picture of his life, because he played a significant role not only in the development of New Spanish history but also in U.S. history as well. When the United States acquired northern Mexico, it did not acquire a barren wasteland but one that was relatively settled with sophisticated infrastructures already intact, especially in California with its coastal settlements and network of missions, forts and ranches. Jose Joaquin took part in both the establishment and settlement of one of the stronger and more successful regions of California – San Francisco.

He enlisted in the military when he was fifteen years old. In the early part of his career, the military placed him on the northern frontiers of New Spain, where he interacted with Pima and Apache natives. He was involved in forming diplomatic relations with them, as well as violently suppressing any rebellions, of which there were many. Achieving the rank of lieutenant, life for Jose was probably difficult. Spain was suffering economically, and frontier outposts and forts were not a priority for crown spending. In addition to patrolling, he spent much of his time maintaining crops and livestock in and around the presidios. Resources had become so scarce that many times survival on frontier outposts depended on their own harvests and livestock. Therefore, Jose's early life in Pimeria Alta, the region where he was stationed, was likely more that of a farmer or rancher than anything else. However, he would go on to become a pivotal explorer and settler by the late eighteenth century.

Prior to the military exploratory expeditions in 1770s, Franciscan friars such as Father Junipero Serra, who is known to be one of the harshest of "conquerors" in this region by forcing religion violently on California's natives, constructed missions with the help of settlers and the indigenous. The primary goals of these missions were to aid in establishing a Spanish presence within unsettled areas of the empire, conversion, and to expand mission and therefore Spanish influence. At first, soldiers were usually stationed within these missions to provide protection. However, as relationships with natives became more secure, the military treated them more harshly. But larger missions and ones of more strategic importance still needed protection, so presidios were constructed near them where the military would be housed. By the 1770s, Russia, England, and later the United States, who were quick to exploit any new resources they could find in the West, prompted the Spanish settlement of current-day northern California.

The De Anza Expedition and the Ohlone

FOLLOWING EARLIER HISTORICAL PATTERNS, throughout the 1700s frontier missions and presidios had to survive and function autonomously. More demanding taxation on Spanish colonies continued to finance wars in Europe and rendered resources limited for colonists, especially in the isolated regions of the north. Moreover, since roads through California were scarce and difficult to navigate, these missions and presidios had to rely on ships and mule transportation to supply them. To allow for wider settlement in the Alta California region, presidios were also constructed along roads to ensure the safe transportation of goods throughout the region and for communication to the capital. In 1770, Gaspar de Portola founded a presidio in present-day Monterrey (Monte Rey after the name given to it by Sebastian Viscaino who first explored the coastline of northern California by boat) and laid the plans for

Moraga Deconstructed

the Mission San Carlos De Barromeo on his second expedition. Juan Bautista De Anza led permanent Spanish settlers to the present-day San Francisco area from 1775–1776. Lieutenant Jose Joaquin Moraga accompanied him.

De Anza and, to some extent, Jose Joaquin, are known as the founders of the San Francisco Presidio, which was erected to protect the Mission San Francisco de Asis and other missions later on. Some Moraga enthusiasts claim Jose Joaquin actually founded the fort but officially, according to Spanish record, De Anza led the expedition so therefore he did. Some point to accounts purported to have been written by Moraga himself, but he was illiterate. Most of his history was actually recorded by Fray Pedro Font, the Franciscan priest who accompanied Moraga on his journey. That being stated, De Anza left within sixteen days of the presidio being founded according to the De Anza journal. Regardless of whether Jose Joaquin led the expedition or actually was the "official" founder, it was he who was left to command the San Francisco presidio for years after De Anza left, overseeing civil engineering projects and forming relationships with the Ohlone natives that lived in the areas surrounding the fort.

Both the De Anza and Moraga names are peppered throughout the presidio area of San Francisco today. De Anza's Historic Trail, which starts in Nogales, Mexico, goes through it. There is a Moraga Hall in the main complex of the presidio and a "Calle Moraga" that is on the main grounds in the main post area. Throughout the city of San Francisco, there are streets named after De Anza and Moraga as well, which gives an idea just how historically important the two figures were and still are to the area.

Given that there was such a small band of people – almost 300 – who were mostly unarmed at the Presidio, peaceful diplomacy probably had to be the basis for early Spanish and Ohlone tribe relationships since the Monterrey presidio was hours away by horse or mule, musketry was scarce, and there were little provisions. This is by no means an attempt of to detract from the horrors associated with Spanish colonization that were likely inflicted on the Ohlone and other native inhabitants through the cruelty of the Catholic church and the Spanish military. Yet given their predicament of being isolated, Jose Joaquin and the settlers likely vied for securing stability with the surrounding natives for survival. At least in the beginning, these interactions had to be more peaceful than violent because the presidio's existence required interaction and trade with the Ohlone to survive. Stated by Jose Joaquin in the account of the founding of San Francisco:

"It was now very late and my supplies were getting low, for which reason I decided before they were [completely] used up to go to explore the river and seek a ford by which to pass from one side to the other, and at the same time to see if I might discover its source. Then an unusual thing happened to me with the Indians of those villages. It was this. When they saw me seeking a crossing over the river, without my asking them a single thing they showed me a ford by which with ease I was able to pass from one side to the other, they themselves going ahead of the horses serving as guides, an action for which I thanked them and for which I attempted to reward them with glass beads, a present much esteemed by them. It is certain that these and the rest of the Indians whom I encountered while my exploration lasted I found affable, generous, and not at all mistrustful of communication with us." [38]

Jose Ignacio Moraga—The Apache in Pimeria Alta

LIVING AT ROUGHLY THE SAME TIME as Lt. Jose Joaquin Moraga was Jose Ignacio Moraga, who commanded the presidio at Tubac in the 1790s, near present-day Tucson, Arizona. There is little written on Jose Ignacio other than his possible sibling relationship to Jose Joaquin and his experiences in Arizona, which were indeed unique compared to his supposed brother's. It is within the context of the Spanish encroaching into North American Apache territory that Jose Ignacio Moraga will be explored.

The Tubac presidio existed in a volatile environment in the present-day region of Tucson during the Apache-Mexican wars.[39] Though the name of the wars imply severity, during Jose Ignacio's command of the Tubac presidio, there was not so much outright violence as there was a state of constant friction.[40]

By the late 1700s, the Spanish made peace with the Pimas and Yuma that lived in the Pimeria Alta, but the various tribes and subtribes of the Apache remained hostile to the Spanish at the Tubac presidio. The Apache tribes were not originally from the

Tubac region but were nomadic and relied on hunting and raiding other tribes to exist, particularly the Sobaipuri tribe in the latter half of the 1700s.[41] Most tribes in the region could not solely rely on agrarian living because of the harsh desert climate; so nomadic life was necessary for survival.

"Gifting" was a "soft" pacification tactic used by the Spanish to make native tribes reliant on them and later to promote trade relations. The Sobaipuri were one of many tribes that became dependent on the Spanish presidios for gifts which, during this time, were essentially used to buy loyalty and came in many forms such as food, European goods, metals, weapons and agricultural goods. The Apache took advantage of this by raiding the Sobaipuri and other tribes that traded with the Spanish; as a result consistently raided tribes moved closer to presidio borders for protection and the easier access to trade. As the years progressed, the Tubac presidio consistently had to intervene in Apache raids on the Sobaipuri. Ironically, because of periods of supply shortages in the late 1700s, the Presidio military also began to raid native tribe settlements, thereby contributing to the volatile environment surrounding the presidio.

The soldiers of Pimeria Alta were different from soldiers in Europe and colonial regulars further south in New Spain toward the capital. Being in the desert, they had to fight in dry climates on hilly terrain. Heavy armor and arms proved more of a hindrance than help. Rifles were common, although on the northern frontiers there was a lack of them because they were expensive, and ammunition was hard to come by. Soldiers usually fought on horseback to compete with the mounted warriors of aggressive tribes. They wore thick leather armor, as it was lighter and protected against arrows, the natives' weapon of choice. Muskets, javelins, short swords, and knives were widely utilized. Despite the technological advantage the Spanish held over the Apaches, the latter had larger numbers of warriors and were more familiar with the terrain. Throughout the eighteenth century and into the nineteenth century, battles between the Spanish and the Apache left hundreds on both sides dead.

Nevertheless, the European approach to settlement continued to rely heavily on subsistence agriculture allowing for the production of farming goods and for ranching livestock especially in the form of cattle. Both became desired commodities among the nomadic natives in the regions and necessary for the budding Spanish mining industry to develop in the Tucson region. As trade increased, traders became priority targets for the Apache who continued to be at odds with the Spanish because of their refusal to convert and to settle. In 1788, Captain Jose Romero of the Tucson presidio was killed during Apache unrest, and Lt. Jose Ignacio Moraga assumed control until 1791. During this period, Ignacio formed diplomatic affiliations with the Avairaipa Apache tribe, who were the first Apache sub-tribe to do so with the Spanish in the Tucson region.[42] This is remarkable because most of the Apache tribes in the region lived in what they referred to as "Spain's Imaginary Kingdom," which implies that though a Spanish border had been established, in no way was Spanish law or society successfully imposed on the natives in the region, nor would it be for generations. In fact, the Apache were able to keep the Spanish, Mexico, and later the United States from completely settling their domains until the late 1800s.

The Apaches also would play a role in the life of the next Moraga who served in the Union army during the U.S. Civil War, nearly a hundred years later.

Chapter 8
The 1800s

IN ORDER TO ADEQUATELY UNDERSTAND Augustine Moraga and how he lived, the historical timeline of Mexico needs to be understood. Following similar Latin American movements, Mexico gained its independence from Spain in 1821 after a class uprising. The rebellion that formed that contributed to Mexican independence was in response to new French Bourbon control of Spain and its colonies. To establish itself after it gained sovereignty, Mexico needed to borrow significantly from France. The eventual default on loans caused the French to intervene militarily and administratively in Mexican affairs for decades after. This eventually forced Mexico to violently rid itself of the French occupation which culminated at the battle of Puebla on May 5, 1862.[43]

Concurrently, the Mexican-American War (also called "Mr. Polk's War," or the "War of American Aggression," as it is known in Mexico) had nearly cut Mexico in half after ceding the northern region to the United States in 1848 under the Treaty of Guadalupe Hidalgo. The populations of these regions, having barely known any type of autonomy for thirty years, were now citizens of a country and in a culture that proved to be vastly different from their own. Thirty years after the Mexican-American War, in the mid-late nineteenth century, the next Moraga will be examined and, once again, the historical context around his life has changed significantly.

Augustine Moraga – Mexican-American Union Soldier
THE TYPICAL AMERICAN NARRATIVE usually states the U.S. Civil

Nikolas Gonzales

War was fought between the American Union and Confederate states over the issue of slavery. Though this is an accurate albeit fairly general description, the war obviously impacted the regions and people of the U.S. differently, but rarely is the impact it had in California and the Arizona territory thoroughly highlighted. Latinos, like many Americans in the United States during the Civil War, depending on where their interests lied, held allegiances on both sides. Many wealthy Mexicans in Texas and many Caribbean Latinos who had invested in the slavery institution sided with the Confederacy, while many "Californios," those Mexican-Americans and their descendants who had lived in California before it became part of United States, sided with the Union.

There were clear cases where Mexican-Americans fought against Mexican-Americans during the Civil War, especially in New Mexico where Confederate Texan influences were particularly strong. Mexican "peonage," a kind of debt slavery, played a major role in loyalties as well.[44] Allegiances aside, Union soldiers of California proved to be instrumental in holding off Texas's invasion of southwestern Union territories under the Confederate flag.

During the Civil War, the Confederacy wanted to cause instability in the Southwest by fomenting insurgencies within the Union-loyal areas of what is now California, Arizona and New Mexico. Discontented settlers and Native American tribes that previously had been a source of hostility since the Spanish invaded their lands were encouraged to rise up. Because of this threat, in 1861, the Union recruited volunteers and cavalrymen to occupy parts of the Southwest in a pre-emptive response to any Confederate plans to attack Union territories and to address any potential Native American uprisings. During the latter years of the American Civil War, California's 1st Calvary, which included Augustine Moraga, did most of its fighting in Arizona against the Apaches. Although Augustine would go on to desert the Union army, examination of why he did so may shed light on Californian and Mexican-American outlooks and attitudes in the Union military.

To understand Augustine Moraga's particular military context and eventual desertion, one must conceptualize the clear changes in Mexican-American status that came with the conquest of Mexican California. That Augustine Moraga was recruited to the 1st Cavalry of California meant he was likely a Californio rancher from Northern California, which was one of the more culturally diverse parts of the United States at the time. White Protestants, whose roots usually were on the East Coast, held much of the wealth and elite status, while native Americans, Afro-Americans, Asians, Mexican settlers, along with, Californios and Mexican-Americans, all formed the lower social classes.

Though part of the Union, the region did not totally embrace the East Coast's policies of tolerance and abolition. Neither did it readily enforce abolitionist ideals of equality where Mexicans and Native Americans were concerned. Brendan Lindsay, in his preface of *Murder State: California's Native American Genocide, 1846-1873*, states that "…Self-described hard-working, self-sufficient, entrepreneurial citizens claimed they were doing their pragmatic best to bring peace, order, and law in the name of the democracy, progress, and the fulfillment of Manifest Destiny by killing or relocating uncivilized savages in California."[45]

Given this atmosphere, and the fact that the Mexican-American War ended about a decade and a half earlier, many Mexicans, Native Americans, poor settlers, and Californios did not embrace the sovereignty of the United States, much like many hadn't embraced the legitimacy of the French or Spanish crown in the years before. By the American Civil War, many of the Mexican landowners, who were inexperienced with new American judicial system, saw their land slowly stripped away from them through the California Land Act of 1851. The Act for the Government and Protection of Indians allowed white Americans to buy Native Americans into servitude.[46] These combined with the unlawful lynching of Californios, like Manuel Vera in 1863—who was illegally dragged from a Northern California jail and then hanged—perpetuated a lack of confidence in the legal system among Mexican-Americans.

Also, shortly before the American Civil War began, Southern California attempted to establish itself as its own sovereign territory and planned to leave the Union, so it shouldn't be a surprise that some residents empathized with the Southern states, particularly Texas, which seceded in 1861. However, when secession came to be seen as an act of war by the Union, and the fact that the remaining French in Mexico sided with the Confederate states, attitudes toward the Union shifted.

Many of the Californios who volunteered for the Union military probably did not share the same patriotic zeal with the soldiers in the ranks of the Civil War's eastern theaters. Rather than join out of a sense of duty to their country, the typical Californio or Mexican-born Union soldier saw the military as a chance at upward mobility and economic stability more than anything else. Allegiance might not have played as big of an idealistic role as it did for Americans in the north and in the south.

Amid the friction between these groups, in Placerville, California—a small town just outside of present-day Sacramento—Augustine Moraga volunteered for the California 1st Cavalry on May 16, 1864. He was a part of the last volunteer group to fill out the four companies being sent to Arizona under Brigadier General Andres Pico. Augustine trained for a month before he mustered out from the Presidio in San Francisco June of that same year,[47] and shipped to Arizona soon after.

Arizona, then a territory, was in disarray. By the U.S. Civil War, many native Apaches in this region became increasingly at odds with non-Apache settlers. The U.S. government had set up an overland mail route that aided in the American settlement of the territory, but by 1864 it was abandoned because of the constant raiding by the "Chiricahua" Apache tribes. Many Americans and their businesses left the Arizona territory along the mail route. Afraid of the Confederacy taking advantage of this situation, Union soldiers were sent to quell the Apache uprisings and to fend off any potential Confederate threats,[48] as well as be in an advantageous position should the French try to reoccupy parts of the northern territories Mexico had lost during the Mexican-American war. Be that as it may, many of the soldiers of the 1st Cavalry were left grossly underprovisioned in the hot Arizona desert towards the end of the Civil War.

Augustine would only see service in the Union military for seventeen months. On August 11, 1865, records indicate that he was one of four soldiers to have deserted at Antelope Peak.[49] Why he left remains a mystery.

It took a considerable length of time to gather the numbers for Company B, Moraga's company, and the regiment had only completed a month of training before mustering out. It would seem more than likely that the Union would have had to insist upon taking almost anyone who volunteered, including those unfit for duty.

The seemingly strongest reason for desertion given the precedence of treatment of Californios by the U.S. government would probably be, as stated above, the lack of military supplies and support in the Arizona territory. By summer 1865, the California cavalry had marched to the Arizona territory in an effort to suppress the Apache uprisings, to reinforce the Union presence, and to offer protection of the overland mail route during its reconstruction. There, soldiers suffered from insufficient food, supplies, and provisions and had hardly any Union regulars to aid them.

Andrew Masiche writes in his The Civil War in Arizona: The Story of the California Volunteers, 1861–1865:

"Morale among the Californians in Arizona reached a low point in late 1865 and early 1866. As the war wound down in the east so did the zeal of the volunteer troops (California Cavalry). Manning forts, patrolling the Mexican border and remaining on the lookout for die-hard Rebels became the tasks of the fresh regiments. But most of these men could not wait until the day came for their final discharge from service."[50]

The Mexican-American's relationship with the United States would continue to change into the twentieth century. The next Moraga we'll discuss was also a soldier, in World War II, and the following chapter will examine both his life and his community in Los Angeles during pivotal labor movements.

Chapter 9
Mexican-Americans and the Labor Movements of Los Angeles

The Mexican-American in the Twentieth Century

DURING THE TWENTIETH CENTURY, the United States became the country we know today. From Maine to California, it had two coasts with access to both Europe and Asia, and territories including Puerto Rico, Hawaii and Alaska (the last two would become states in 1959). Booming cities across the country benefited from both industrial might and newfound economic prosperity. Throughout the earlier years of the 1900s, Mexican-Americans played a role in bolstering this growth and contributed to the effort in the first and second world wars, but Mexican-Americans were still considered by many to be second-class citizens on the West Coast. This prompted a rise in their political awareness and action during the first half of the twentieth century.

Despite their absorption into American society, many Latinos continued to occupy the lower rungs of the socioeconomic ladder. Although situations improved in the American Southwest, economic mobility was difficult for many, which led to the early stages of organized labor movements in Los Angeles, the epicenter for the Mexican-American political movements in the twentieth century. The next Moraga, my grandfather Edward, will be examined during this time. Although Edward was not known for any particular political contribution, his experience embodied the ideological and social struggles unique to Mexican-Americans when viewed through the lens of the early labor movements.

Edward Moraga, Los Angeles, and World War II

IN THE EARLY YEARS OF THE TWENTIETH CENTURY, when America prospered during the Gilded Age, the southwest and western regions of the United States and its diverse populations existed in relative isolation compared to most of the country. Politically, the area had strong ties to Mexico. Many elite and educated Mexicans organized and recruited for the Mexican Revolution in Los Angeles.[51] Many living on the American side worked and conducted business in Mexico as well. The border was porous.

Edward Moraga was born in California on April 30, 1923, and as a child was a migrant farm worker traveling between Mexico and the United States. He worked the fields of Los Angeles, San Fernando Valley, at farms outside San Diego, and in Tijuana and Ensenada, Mexico. Edward attended school in Mexico and throughout California, eventually graduating from high school in Los Angeles. Like many of the men in his family, he was drafted into the Second World War. His military service consisted of loading ordinance onto bomber aircraft in Britain. When the war ended, Edward shipped home to Los Angeles and started a family with his high school sweetheart, Dolores, and later worked for the railway company Amtrak as an upholsterer. He retired in 1988 and died in December 2011.

Although he may not have been aware of it, Edward and the other Los Angeles Latinos of his generation were part of labor force that helped sow the seeds of revolutionary political and social movements for Mexican-Americans in the United States. This helped influence a shift in consciousness that later helped usher in the Civil Rights Movements in the 1960s and paved the way for Latino social equality.

During Edward's youth, Latinos, like many other ethnic minorities and immigrants, became scapegoats for the United States' economic instability after the stock market crash of 1929. His community was particularly targeted as "feeding off the system" by "taking American" jobs, even though they were legally Americans. Many of them were Californios whose families had been in the United States for generations. Despite this, local governments urged companies not to hire Latinos, and to fire them without cause after the crash.

Border checkpoints strictly enforced new U.S. entry policies from 1929 until the end of World War II. This was very different from the World War I years, when Mexicans were welcomed as migrants to the United States, providing labor for shortages caused by the war. This changed during the Hoover and Roosevelt administrations when there was little regard for the citizenship status of the masses of Latinos who were illegally deported across the border to Mexico, leaving families behind throughout the United States[52] in what is commonly referred to as the "Mexican Repatriation." Although Edward and his family were not deported to Mexico, many in his community were.

As Edward entered into his late teens, he saw his community continually targeted. He witnessed the injustice of the Sleepy Lagoon trials in summer 1942 and while doing his U.S. military service, he heard about the Zoot Suit Riots that erupted in 1943[53] when hundreds of American military men, from the same military in which he was enlisted, incited race violence throughout the streets of Los Angeles by unlawfully arresting and beating "Zoot Suiter" Mexican-American youth, as well as other minority groups, with police help. (Zoot suits were a popular baggy style of clothing for Latinos in Los Angeles, which consisted of tapered baggy slacks, wallet chain, hat with feather, dress shirt, and jacket.) With the crackdown on Zoot Suiters, Edward saw his community again scapegoated, labeled as anti-patriotic and un-American…simply for the clothes they wore. However, despite these attacks against Latinos, Edward willingly continued serving in the U.S. Army.

The Labor Movements of Los Angeles in Edward Moraga's Youth

THERE WAS MORE TO THE STRONG CHICANO COMMUNITIES of Los Angeles than cultural cohesion. Los Angeles, with a deep-rooted history of Latino pride, also had been the nexus of Mexican-American political thought and action since the early 1900s. With strong ties to the Mexican government during the U.S. Civil War and into the Mexican Revolution, the Los Angeles Latino communities encouraged the exchange of ideas with reform activists like Ricardo Flores Magon and Pascual Orozco, who were influential in Mexican revolutionary thought. Because of their access to Mexican thinkers, community leaders in Los Angeles were very familiar with organizational and institutional reform and politicking.

Edward's family was involved with contractual agricultural work throughout California and Mexico, so they benefited from Los Angeles's organized labor strikes of the 1930s and 1940s, which were based on a combination of Mexican, American, feminist, and communist ideas. These strikes helped solidify and unite the different institutional communities and left a long-lasting impression within the southern California region and on its Latin-American communities.

One of the first labor protests that helped to "puncture the idea of Mexican docility"[54] (and firmly establish some of the first Latino unions in Southern California) was the El Monte Berry Pickers strike of 1933, which started in the Hicks Camp outside of El Monte, California, a suburb in Los Angeles's San Gabriel Valley. It spread across the region to Culver City, more than thirty miles away, and although many considered the strike a failure, it still ignited widespread Latino labor unionization. John Laslet states in *The Sunshine was Never Enough: Los Angeles Workers 1880-2010*, "The strikers at El Monte, like other Mexican immigrant workers who labored in the sweater trades, were groping for a new sense of identity that was an amalgam of many elements, some drawn for their Mexican heritage and some from their U.S. experience."[55]

Another indicator of growing Mexican-American labor reform in Los Angeles occurred in 1939 when the first Latino civil rights organization in Southern California, known as "El Congreso del Pueblo de Habla Espanola," formed. It would become so influential that it eventually developed organizational ties with the Congress of Industrial Organization (CIO) and the American Federation of Labor (AFL). With the help of leaders and political thinkers like communist Dorothy Healey and feminist Luisa Moreno, Los Angeles agricultural and industrial institutions organized multiple strikes throughout the region with the help of "Congreso."

These strikes generated better workers' rights and education, more gender equality in the workplace, political influence and awareness, and promoted union cohesion among Mexican-Americans by encouraging them to take labor stances alongside other ethnic counterparts and white Americans as well. Laslet states, "Built around the leadership skills of Luisa Moreno and Josefina Fierro de Bright, El Congreso put together a remarkable coalition of Mexican Union organizers, civil rights activists, and social justice groups, including the Workers Alliance, the Women's International League for Peace and Freedom, and a group of left-wing Hollywood artists and writers from the Screen Actors Guild. This new movement toward cross-cultural and cross-gender solidarity would become even stronger when it was reinforced by the industrial union philosophy of the CIO."[56]

This changed the political and social landscape to which Edward Moraga returned.

Back from the War

AFTER WORLD WAR II, the political context of Latino communities in Los Angeles changed, as did the attitudes of many their members who returned home from the war. Observable social inequality and work abuse still existed in post war Los Angeles, but Edward, having been a former laborer and now former soldier, understood that social and educational opportunities that promoted mobility now existed more than ever before, and he pursued them. Moreover, remnants of the labor movements that happened during Edward's youth and ongoing movements that started while he was at war prompted a change in his political outlook[57] providing the required space needed for him to seek economic mobility and equality.

Edward's pursuit of an education and his later decisions to open a business and to unionize after his return to the United States show this. Since he loved mathematics and accounting,[58] he went to school for the latter when he moved back to Los Angeles. But, having five children, he unfortunately could not dedicate the time necessary to complete his studies.[59] He also went into business as a restaurateur with his brother Robert Moraga, but because of his lack of experience in the private sector, this did not grow to fruition either. Later, when he worked for the furniture company Restwell as an assembler, he helped to organize for unionization— this is supposedly why both he and his wife Dolores were fired from the company.[60]

These efforts mark a switch in perspective, which again likely came from the confidence Edward gained in the military and the context into which he was reinserted when he returned from the war. Though Mexican-American communities in Los Angeles were still suffering socio-economically, they were stronger and more empowered and emphasized entrepreneurship, equality, education and ideas brought about by Los Angeles labor movements. Having spent his youth suffering in an institution fraught with unfair workers' rights and maltreatment only to go on to war for a country that, in his experience, consistently targeted his community, then to return home from war to a strengthened but still disregarded community…must have been a profoundly challenging ordeal. At the same time the new political climate promoted an observable sense of hope and opportunity, enough to pursue a career, an education, and the sense of purpose to unionize. The next Moraga will establish herself in a complex time as well but confronted different challenges relating to identity awareness, gender, and sexual orientation.

Chapter 10
The Contemporary Chicana Artist

THE MEXICAN-AMERICAN, or "Chicano" (a term adopted during the Chicano movement of the 1960s), in the twenty-first century exists in a considerably different context than even that of the late twentieth century. Advocacy organizations and civil rights groups, including the League of United Latin American Citizens (LULAC), the Movimiento Estudiantil Chicano de Aztlan (MECHA), and the Mexican American Political Association (MAPA) exist. Equal opportunity policies have been pushed to promote diversity in the workplace and in education. Through legislation, which no doubt was brought about by some of the aforementioned organizations and movements in the previous chapter, the opportunities for the Chicano are now more plentiful. But the Chicano/Chicana of the twenty-first century faces a different set of obstacles that relate more to their identities, specifically understanding and embracing them.

From experience, it seems many Chicanos from the Los Angeles area today exist in a divided world, one where they speak Spanish with relatives but refrain from speaking Spanish in public. They pronounce their Spanish name in an English accent in front of non-Latinos and think that America has more to do with shaping them than their Latino and/or native backgrounds, even though their family histories in all likelihood followed a very distinctive path compared to other Americans. These Mexican-Americans no longer only live in "barrios," and many have completely assimilated to American life and diffused into other communities in the middle, upper-middle, and upper classes. Chicanos, for lack of a better term, are obtaining the "American" dream. Albert

Moraga Deconstructed

Amandirez Sr., former president of LULAC, believed Mexican-Americans in the late twentieth and early twenty-first centuries were dealing with the issue of being "torn between two desires- the desire to be good to our brothers who come across the borders and suffer so much when they are here trying to get ahead and our desire to have those that are here as citizens advance in our society and become better adjusted to American life with the benefits of American life."[61]

Like other ethnic minorities living in the United States, Chicanos often find themselves in a cultural limbo of not being fully accepted by either Mexican or American cultures. Extremes at times come into play. To some native Mexicans, they are considered "Pochos," which is a derogatory term given to Mexicans born in the United States and more or less means "sell out." To many white Americans, Chicanos are a hybrid that should embrace more of the American aspect of their identity rather than their Latino one.

Giving into cultural pressures, it seems some contemporary Chicanos associate more with U.S. culture rather than their Mexican or other native cultures, seeming to shun their historical identity believing it has little to do with them. In a sense, it isn't that they have forgotten where they come from, but rather some ignore their heritages because they're indirectly taught, or feel, they are a part of something "better" now. Sadly, some are completely unaware of this and "do not know what they do not know." It is not the opinion of the author that anyone is to blame for this or that this is *wrong*, but many times current American history courses, especially at the primary level, mostly reinforce typical historical narratives that perpetuate an American "oneness" in an effort to reinforce a solidified political identity. It is ironic that the United States is nominally a place that prides itself on diversity, yet in practice only promotes a monolithic culture.

Some Chicanos in the early twenty-first century might view themselves as being culturally different from other Americans, but even when they do, they may not celebrate it or feel it is appropriate. General perceptions of Chicanos tend to veer toward the culturally inferior side of the social spectrum with political trends in such areas as illegal immigration contributing to this.

Nikolas Gonzales

Without an emphasis on the important historical contributions made by Mexicans and Mexican-Americans in the United States, which seem only to be observable in higher education, the contemporary Chicano rarely sees public acknowledgement of the fact that they are a people, who have achieved and struggled for hundreds of years, as a mix of Americans, natives, Mexicans, Africans or Europeans. Today, they exist as a conquered but proud and enduring people within the United States who have been culturally evolving alongside and within the country for hundreds of years on their own historical path. These factors carry with them implications that mark the Chicano experience as different from any other culture living in the Americas.

Cherrie Moraga Lawrence addresses this cultural struggle through the perspectives of a writer, Chicana feminist, and lesbian of both American and Mexican descent. Since the late 1970s, she has been indirectly active in the Queer movement by carving her place among U.S. literary communities as one of the most prolific writers in her arenas. Her ideas about identity politics and her place in American society have been highly influential in Latin American studies, Chicano studies, American literature, and theater. She is currently on faculty at the University of California Santa Barbara English department.

Cherrie Moraga Lawrence

CHERRIE MORAGA LAWRENCE was born in Whittier, California, in 1952 to Joseph Lawrence and Vera Moraga. She was raised in the San Gabriel Valley, outside of downtown Los Angeles, earned her undergraduate degree from Immaculate Heart College and her graduate degree from San Francisco State University. In California's Bay Area during the late 1970s, she started writing poetry and became politically active. Her writing on the feminist experience, gender and class embody the late twentieth and early twenty-first century contemporary struggle for Chicano/Chicana identity in the Southwest. She also views her ideas on gender equality and sexual orientation through a lens of existing in two cultures, which contributes to a very particular dynamic.

There were specific social factors at play that enabled Cherrie to articulate her thoughts on these matters that in another time may have been silenced.

As a child, Cherrie saw monumental changes in civil rights awareness and political and social thought, but unlike Edward Moraga, she has said she was keenly aware of it.[62] The Cold War, the Civil Rights Movement, and the anti-Vietnam war movements profoundly affected American society and promoted a major change in perceptions of African-American equality, war, and the U.S. government. Eventually, other underrepresented minorities and groups were affected, prompting a series of cultural revolutions. All of this occurred during Cherrie's formative years, which encouraged her (along with many other Americans) to explore their own identities on several levels. This was especially evident in her writings that dealt with being a closeted lesbian in a conservative Chicano family[63] within the larger patriarchal Latino communities of Los Angeles.

Along with the United Kingdom, the United States moved toward progressive legislation and social reform for gays in the 1960s and 1970s. In 1969, the Stonewall Riots in New York City marked one of the most important events in the Gay Liberation Movement and is celebrated internationally every year with gay pride parades in major cities. The first national gay rights conference was held in 1973. In 1974, the first national lesbian conference took place in Canterbury. In 1977, Harvey Milk became the first openly gay elected official in the United States when he was elected to the San Francisco board of supervisors and helped formulate progressive legislation for homosexual rights in Northern California.

By the time Cherrie's work found popularity in the early 1980s, the Gay Rights Movement (GRM) in the Bay Area was already gaining considerable momentum. Although she identified with it to an extent, she felt she contributed to the movement more as an artist rather than an activist.[64] The movement developed through what Cherrie refers to as "different phases of consciousness" and felt that as a woman of color at some point she began to identify less with the GRM because it was becoming a movement mostly associated with elite white men, some of whom she believed were misogynists.[65]

Much like prolific writer Audrey Lorde, who wrote

extensively on the Afro-American feminist queer struggle, Cherrie wrote literature focusing specifically on the Chicana's experience. Her groundbreaking work, collaborating with Gloria Anzaldua in 1981, was *This Bridge Called My Back,* which Cherrie said was a work that is a "complex convergence of identities—race, class, gender, and sexuality—systemic to women of color oppression and liberation."[66] That same year, she helped found Kitchen Table Press in New York City to publish works by women of color and every sexual orientation. This was the first press completely run by female American ethnic minorities and dedicated solely to their writings.

 In contrast to the very first Moraga observed in this book, Arias Moragas, the soldier who went on to conquer in the name of Catholicism in Spain, Cherrie would go on to become an award-winning writer into the twenty-first century and the recipient of numerous fellowships inspiring Chicanos and Chicanas throughout the U.S. In the early years of her career, she won the American Book Award by the Before Columbus Foundation in 1986. She won the Lesbian Rights Award from the organization the Southern California Women of Understanding for outstanding contributions in Lesbian Literature and Service to the Lesbian Community in 1992 and the National Endowment of the Arts Theater Playwright Fellowship in 1993. She won the first annual Cara award from UCLA in 1999 and also won the National Association for Chicana and Chicano Studies Scholars Award, 2001. She would then go on to receive the United States Artist Rockefeller Fellowship for literature in 2007.

Conclusion

FOR A NUMBER OF YEARS, I taught ninth-grade U.S. history and humanities to immigrant English language learners on the East Coast. This was a very specialized student population, mostly new immigrants, limited in their command of English, and not at the same grade level of literacy as American-born students of the same age. Nearly all of them came from lower socioeconomic backgrounds, and some were not even at the proper age/grade literacy levels in their native languages. In addition to teaching history, I was also charged with teaching English as a Second Language in my classes. Theoretically, this approach of learning language through content aids in students acquiring English faster, as opposed to learning solely through English language classes. It usually works.

Sadly, in the sphere of American education, this specific population is highly marginalized. In impoverished neighborhoods, newly immigrated students are even less of a priority in public education than their American counterparts. I wasn't given adequate teaching materials and offered little guidance by school administrators. For example, I had only a history textbook designed for fifth graders to teach my *ninth* graders, who were between the ages of thirteen and twenty-two. Other than observing the mandatory teaching standards, it was mostly my task as an educator to formulate content curriculum for my students, which was difficult considering that most teachers have a solid curriculum already written for them that they must follow.

But I loved my students. My experience with them enlightened me to the power of the discipline of history, its vastly different interpretations, and its use as a tool to instill cultural identity and self-confidence. Having knowledge of oneself makes one a better-informed person promoting a larger sense of purpose as human beings and as citizens.

But since my students came from a myriad of backgrounds, mainly Latino, I could not lecture the entire class in English and expect them—especially the younger ones—to internalize the complex ideas of history and perform well. I could not expect them to read up on and retain certain subject matter on their own because grasping the abstract theories in an entirely different language is difficult, if not impossible, for students who just entered the country and had no English skills. I had to write curriculum that would suit their abilities.

There was no baseline to work from. I had to differentiate my lessons for each class, provide ample individualized attention to each of my students, and utilize my foreign language abilities to teach. As I honed my craft and realized the different approaches required to teach my students, I questioned whether they actually learned the concepts I taught or were just memorizing and regurgitating to placate me. I constantly heard fellow faculty say that "kids are kids" and "students are students," and although I knew many of the kids liked me and wanted to impress me, I also knew many of them just wanted to stop me from hounding them for their homework. No matter how much I tailored the instruction for them, I began to realize that they were not learning history through the same lens I had. Unlike students educated in the United States, they did not grow up understanding the history of their new country, and they weren't immersed in communities that promoted it. I believe many did their work out of simple fear of being in a new school and to conform.

As I strived to cater to the needs of my students, I reflected on my own cultural heritage as a Chicano born male, raised, and educated in the United States. Having grown up in Los Angeles, I was a Mexican-American living in a largely Latino city; my identity was never an issue for me. As far as I could see, I was just another American growing up in the United States. When I began to travel in my twenties, living in other American cities and outside of the United States, I began to realize how being Mexican-American was unlike being any other type of ethnic minority from my country, and that each and every minority has his or her own distinct experience.

As I pleaded to my ninth-grade students to know their own culture, to never let go of it, and to cherish their history, I realized that because I had not been fully aware of my cultural identity at their age that I ,their teacher, lived in a cultural limbo. I was exactly what I did not want my students to become. Sure, I knew the "American" past of the Mexican-American side of my hybrid culture but the Mexican side wasn't emphasized in school. I could see that U.S. history, as it is commonly presented, promotes the mythical idea that everyone who is American only has an *American* history, which, again, isn't the case at all. America is an idea, an excellent one, but has always been a country of immigrants with their own experiences. So, in addition to U.S. history, I started to teach the students histories from their countries and designed lessons that focused on how the different cultures in my classes contributed in their own way to the past of the U.S. I found the common ground.

This engaged my students. This *worked*. I took this learning strategy and applied it to this book.

The close examination of the Moraga family name over the centuries has been an excellent vehicle to convey a wider history that has been largely overlooked in the U.S. And so, the Mexican-American's chronicle begins in several places at almost the same time, not in New England. We need to look in the Caribbean, in Hispanola, more than 100 years before the English pilgrims landed. Spanish settlers came to the Americas for economic opportunity, to escape the instability Spain was encountering in the 1500s, and for the church to find Catholic converts. This is very different from the so-called pilgrim religious freedom motivation, even though eventually as the New England colonies grew, colonial Americans became just as self-interested as the Spanish conquering and displacing many Native American tribes. As the Spanish intermingled with the native cultures and introduced African slaves as a source of labor into the New World, this gave rise to new and distinct social systems that have echoed into today.

The Spanish then moved on to conquer present-day North America, Central America, and South America throughout the sixteenth century, setting up a series of vice-royalties that composed the colonies of "New Spain." Soldiers conquered the Mexica tribes, and from there Spanish power spread in virtually all directions. Some lands became more settled than others. Alta California, present-day West and Southwest region of the United States, was inhospitable and remained largely unexplored until the late 1700s. Non-Spanish European merchants, shippers, and hunters sought these unsettled lands, prompting Spain to populate these territories more heavily. In an effort to do this, the crown, along with the church and natives, built presidios and mission networks focusing on the present-day California coastline with its fertile coasts that could be used for agriculture, potential trading ports to Asia, and a growing otter pelt industry.

The Spanish eventually would come to settle this region through the use of the military and conversion, but it would only remain New Spain until the colony gained independence in 1821 becoming Mexico. The new nation faced the internal turmoil of becoming a state along with fending off continual foreign interests, particularly France and the United States. In 1848, Mexico lost nearly half of its land to the U.S. following the Mexican-American War. Within the course of twenty-seven years, the land of the American Southwest changed hands three times. Obviously, the natives and settlers already living in this region faced a difficult time adapting and finding allegiance to any particular government.

Much like during Spanish and Mexican rule, new cultures and communities developed in the U.S. West and Southwest, and some of the most politically active from the mid-nineteenth century onward were in California. Mexican-American communities, probably because of their size, cohesiveness and solidarity, became marginalized as they grappled for their place in American society into the 1900s. By the late twentieth and into the twenty-first centuries, the issues that Chicano communities faced was a lack of awareness of their full political and historical identity and understanding their continuing struggles for a place within American society as ethnic minorities.

So, to end, though this work started with the goal of tracing my grandfather's family history, it evolved into a historical experiment, attempting to expose the past of a major minority and its contributions to the United States. It represents only one of the countless paths Mexican-American history takes, but its aim is to show how the experiences of even one Latino living in the United States is actually part of a sea of rich, vast cultures. Every ethnic group that becomes acculturated and assimilates into a society goes through their own peaks and valleys, with processes that deserve to be explored. It is only when we abandon the idea that various ethnic populations have contributed to U.S. history that injustice occurs. As topics in the hard sciences and business are continually being put at the forefront of education, it has become difficult to address the shortcomings of humanities studies. Therefore, one of the goals of this work is to convey that history cannot and should not continue to be studied and taught in a vacuum and that post-colonial and post-modern approaches to it should start before higher education as early as elementary school.

Separate analyses of various ethnicities *alongside* U.S. history allows for the examination of cultural evolutions as interactions between internal and external forces rather than a single, autonomous political identity that developed solely from the Brits who landed in North America's east coast. One needs to understand that the U.S. did not evolve into *modern splendor* on its own. There is a need for observation of this idea through varying lenses, to peel back critical layers so we can understand the diverse historical patterns that might not otherwise be explored or celebrated.

Appendix

Obstacles

ALTHOUGH THIS BOOK'S FOCUS was at first genealogical in nature, it has evolved to be an analysis of various histories from Europe, the Caribbean, Latin America, and the United States. Its original goal was to examine the shared lineage of Edward and Jose Joaquin Moraga's family members whose ancestors were said to have settled throughout New Spain and Mexico and would go on to settle into what is now present day northern California. These members were known as the original "Californios," those Spanish who came to settle in territorial California in the late eighteenth century. They include José Joaquin Moraga, the Spanish lieutenant who was vital in settling the Presidio in San Francisco in the late 1700s, and his brother Jose Ignacio Moraga, a lieutenant who commanded the Tubac Presidio in Arizona at roughly the same time. Descendants of these branches have formed into micro-branches that have families throughout various regions in California. Though various archives, registries, scholarly journals and books have been consulted in the genealogy formulation, unfortunately there was no convincing data that points to any shared lineage between Edward Moraga, my grandfather, and the Moraga Californios mentioned who helped settle northern California. There have been non-scholarly books written on other branches of the Moraga family in California such as *Moraga's Pride* by Sandy Kimball and bits of data scattered across the internet and in religious and historical archives, but nothing I found in any of these proved concrete. With that being said, and given that I am by no means a credited genealogist and very well could be wrong, new motivations prompted research into the Moraga surname.

Through the dead ends of the genealogical research and experiences as a history teacher, I realized that ethnic Latinos born and raised in the United States share a particularly different experience than other Americans, and this is thoroughly underrepresented in public education and the contemporary U.S. historical narrative. Thus, this work changed from genealogical study into an observation of different "Moraga" personalities from the thirteenth century through the contemporary era in order to convey the diverse roles they played, experiences they felt, and how these all have contributed uniquely to history. This will be explained further in the following section.

Reasoning

PRESSING PROBLEMS CONSISTENTLY SURFACED when researching the Moraga name, which caused the abandonment of the genealogical aspect of this work. In this case, the most severe was by the late 1700s there were hundreds, if not thousands, of Moragas living throughout Spain, Asia, Europe, and in the "New World."[67] It is not a common surname, but many Europeans and Hispanics had it by the eighteenth century. There are thousands of Moragas living throughout the world today and to claim they are all related because of the commonality of a surname would be just as preposterous as claiming that those sharing the typical American name "Smith" have the same lineage. In addition, the Moraga clan in its entirety did not move from one place, settle, and then relocate to another, but unfortunately, much of the information available on the family name only really deals with the descendants of Jose Joaquin Moraga that settled in northern California and not much with other Moraga lines.[68] Again, many Moragas were likely in the New World by the late eighteenth century. Immigration patterns across Europe were comprised of families expanding in several directions, advancing and often reversing again throughout Europe, into North Africa, Asia,[69] and to the Americas.

Issues also surfaced when examining the origins of the name Moraga. It's crucial to understand that Spain did not come to exist, as it is known today, until about the late fifteenth century with the rise of the Catholic monarchs Isabella and Ferdinand. Until then, it was a collection of kingdoms with different cultures and peoples who spoke different languages. Spanish, or "Castilliano," as it is often referred to in Spain, was only one of the major languages spoken on the Iberian Peninsula. Also, among it were languages such as Catalan, Basque and Gallaecian, not to mention Mozarabic and Arabic used by the Islamic Moors, who were a significant presence in the Iberian Peninsula for close to 700 years.

Although there were linguistic commonalities among these kingdoms, names were pronounced differently and had different spellings throughout Iberia's regions. There were many that sounded similar to Moraga and were spelled similarly such as Morague, Moragues, Maraga, Zummaraga, De Moragas and Moragas. Many of these still exist today.

One must also consider that names change through time, and it is quite possible that the Californio branch Moraga surname could have as well. It could have altered when Castilliano was adopted as Spain's lingua franca. It also could have changed when Moragas left to the New World after the 1500s and may have willingly changed it on their own. Lastly, and most important (and this cannot be stressed enough), the Catholic Church in New Spain conferred Spanish names on native Americans and African slaves in the New World after Catholic baptism to impose European patrilineal familial lines.[70] Hence, it is very possible that this happened with the Moraga name as well.

The final issue that needs to be mentioned is the pervasiveness of myth and falsity that might have been introduced into the chronology of the Moraga family history after their settlement and rise to prominence in California in the eighteenth and nineteenth centuries. People with common surnames or sometimes overly ambitious would-be genealogists try to insert their lineages into other lineages with the same name in order to enhance family reputations. This may have been the case for the link between Edward Moraga's lineage and Jose Joaquin Moraga's as well. Edward Moraga's parents, grandparents, and great-grandparents are not included anywhere on José Joaquin Moraga's family tree.[71] Some family members claim Edward was related to Jose Ignacio Moraga, who is supposedly the brother of Jose Joaquin Moraga, but there is no hard evidence that suggests this other than online family trees, many of which can be subject to public change.

Therefore, the combination of lack of hard evidence, possible name changes, and potential fictional lineage combinations led to the abandonment of the genealogical pursuit of this work.

On the other hand, the passage of the Moraga name through time is fascinating, enlightening, complex, and as stated earlier, deserves exposure for many reasons. If the goal of learning history is to help to solidify the identity of members of a modern nation state, then indeed the history of the hegemonic elite should be taught, which obviously has been the pattern. However, the study of history has progressed, and this is clearly no longer enough nor is it ethical. Therefore, to reiterate, if the goal of history is to what Lynda Hunt refers to in "Writing History in the Global Era" as "providing the common threads to bind together disparate peoples whether of different ethnic groups, different classes, or different religion,"[72] then shouldn't the current U.S. historical narrative also more willingly acknowledge and embrace the contributions of its ethnic minorities, including those of Latinos, whose members comprise the third largest ethnic group in the United States and whose ancestors lived in a region that consists of one-third of the continental United States? Moreover, shouldn't it also acknowledge that their histories are patently distinct? To address this, this work has evolved into an analysis of individual Moraga personalities within their historical contexts across a span of 800 years. The approach of using a genealogy was unconventional but provided an important personal medium in which I could relay several different non-traditional interpretations of the past allowing the reader to gain a more diverse and holistic idea of what happened rather than just the top-down history that is still all too commonly presented.

Battle of Las Navas De Tolosa Monument in Santa Elena - 2014.

Inquisition symbol in Granada, Spain. Granada was a hotbed for Inquisition activity after the "Reconquista" - 2014.

Sarcophagus of Christopher Columbus, Sevilla Cathedral, Sevilla Spain - 2014.

Granada Old City, capital of the region to which the Moors were confined after the Battle of Las Navas de Tolosa in 1212 - 2014.

Reconstruction of an Ohlone Hut at Mission Dolores, San Francisco, CA -2013.

Tongve Natives and Priest Relief at the San Gabriel Mission, San Gabriel, CA - 2010.

Moraga Street near the Main Post area in the San Francisco Presidio, San Francisco - 2013.

San Francisco Presidio Ruins, San Francisco, CA - 2013.

Father Frank Gonzales, Stepmother Dorothy Gonzales and Sister Dr. Renee Marquez - 2016.

My Grandmother Lupe Contreras and Frank Gonzales and Siblings - 1977.

Rosalinda Moraga and Frank Gonzales Clan - 2018.

The Edward Moraga Clan - Early 2000s.

My Grandfather Edward Moraga and Me - Early 2000s.

Bibliography

Balderamma, Francisco and Raymond Rodriguez. Decade of Betrayal: Mexican Repatriation in the 1930s. University of New Mexico Press, 2006

Barletta, Vincent. Covert Gestures: Crypto-Islamic Literature as Cultural Practice in Early Modern Spain. USA: University of Minnesota Press, 2005.

Barcelo, Amadeo. "The Battle of Las Navas De Tolosa (I): Chronicle of Rodrigo Jiménez De Rada." El Agitador. July 14, 2012. http://www.bajoaragonesa.org/elagitador/la-batalla-de-las-navas-de-tolosa-i-cronica-de-rodrigo-jimenez-de-rada/

"Blasonari Genealogia y Heraldica" Enciclopedia Heráldica y Genealógica Hispano-Americana de Alberto y Arturo García Carraffa. http://www.blasonari.net/apellido.php?id=679

Carr, Mathew. Blood and Faith. UK: The New Press. 2011.

Civil War Data Regiment Personnel Listing. http://www.civilwardata.com/active/hdsquery.dll?Muster?a=24&b=U%3E&c=&d=7&e=21&f=20

"Consejo Superior de Investigaciones Cientificas Patronato Menendez Y Pelayo."

Institucion Gonzalo Fernandez De Oviedo, Catalogo de Pasajeros A Indias Durante Los Siglos XVI, XVII, y XVIII 63.

"Correspondence with Pedro De Nava". University of Arizona

Nikolas Gonzales

Library. http://www.library.arizona.edu/exhibits/desertdoc/aravaipa.htm

Dodson, Julian. Fanaticos, Exiles and the Mexico-U.S. Border: Episodes of Mexican State Reconstruction, 1923-1929. (Dissertation) University of New Mexico. 2015.

Ellison, William Henry. "The Movement for State Division in California, 1849-1860." The Southwestern Historical Quarterly. Vol. Xvii No. 2 (October, 1913): 101-139.

Ferguson, Thomas John and Chip Colwell-Chonthapohn. History is in the Land: Multi-vocal Tribal Traditions in Arizona's San Pedro. University of Arizona Press. April, 2006.

Gutierrez, David. Between Two Worlds: Mexican Immigrants in the United States. Rowman and Littlefield Publishers. 1996.

Higman, B.W. A Concise History of the Caribbean. Cambridge University Press. December, 2010

Hrdlicka, Ales. "Notes on the Indians of Sonora, Mexico." American Anthropologist, Vol. 6. No. 1 (Jan. - Mar., 1904): 51-89.

Hunt, Lynda. Writing History in the Global Era. Norton Publishing. 2014

"Introduction to Inquisition Policies and Proceedings Documents." University of Notre Dame.
https://inquisition.library.nd.edu/collections/RBSC-INQ:COLLECTION/genre/RBSC-INQ:Policies_and_proceedings

Katz, William. "The First American Freedom Fighter". 2012.
http://williamlkatz.com/first-american-freedom-fighter/

Kellog, Susan. Law and the Transformation of Aztec Culture, 1500-1700. University of Oklahoma Press. 2005.

Kimball, Sandy. Moraga's Pride: Rancho Laguna De Los Palos Colorados. Moraga Historical Society. 1st Edition. 1987.

Laslet, John H. M. The Sunshine was Never Enough: Los Angeles Workers 1880-2010. University of California Press. 2014.

Lea, Henry Charles. The Moriscos of Spain: Their Conversion and Expulsion. Praegar. 1901 Ed. 1968.

Lindsay, Brendan C. Murder State: California's Native American Genocide, 1846-1873. University of Nebraska. 2012.

Llull, Ramon. Noel Fallows The Book of the Order of Chivalry. BOYE6. 2013.

Masich, Andrew E. The Civil War in Arizona: The Story of the California Volunteers, 1861–1865. University of Oklahoma Press. 2nd Edition. 2008.

Miller, Darlus. "Hispanos and the Civil War in New Mexico: A Reconsideration". New Mexico Historical Review, 54:2. (April 1979): 105-123.

Moraga, Cherrie. Oral Interview conducted by the author. August 3, 2015.

Moraga, Cherrie. Loving in the War Years: Lo Que Nunca Paso Por Sus Labios. South End Press. Cambridge, MA. 2000.

Moraga, Edward. Oral Interview conducted by the author. August, 2005.

Moraga, Edward Jr. Oral Interview conducted by the author. April 16, 2017.

Moraga, Frank X. Moraga Family History Website. http://www.moragahistory.com/

Moraga, Rosalinda. Oral Interview conducted by the author. November 13, 2015.

Moraga, Jose Joaquin. "Moraga's Account of the Founding of San Francisco". De Anza Web, University of Oregon. http://anza.uoregon.edu/moraga.html

O'Callaghan, Joseph F. A History of Medieval Spain. Cornell University Press. 1983.

Officer, James E. Hispanic Arizona, 1536–1856. University of Arizona Press. 1989.

Penas, Leandro M and Manuela F. Rodriguez "La Guerra Contra Los Apaches Bajo El Mando De Ramon De Castro Y Pedro De Nava En Las Provincias Interiores." Revista de Historia Militar. Instituto De Historia Y Cultura Militar Año Lvi 2012 Núm. 111: 119-157

Perez Jr. Louis A. To Die in Cuba: Suicide and Society. The University of North Carolina Press. February 26, 2007.

Smith, C. Mark. In the Wake of Lewis and Clark: From the Mountains to the Sea. Lulu Publishing Services. March 24, 2015.

Sturtevant, William. Handbook of North American Indians: Languages (Book 17). Smithsonian Institution Scholarly Press. August 2006.

Zinn, Howard. People's History of the United States. Harper Perennial Modern Classics. August 2, 2005.

Endnotes

1 Mijo is Spanish for my "son," and in this case "grandson."
2 "Caliphate" is an Islamic state led by a Caliph or religious/political leader who is the successor to the Islamic prophet Mohammed.
3   Carr p. 25
4   "A corps of professional soldiers paid regular wages proved to be a more valuable instrument of war. Al-Hakam was the first to recruit large numbers of mercenaries, including Berbers and Sudanese Negroes as well as Christians from northern Spain and even from beyond the Pyrenees." O'Callaghan p. 148
5   "The Reconquista" was expulsion of the Islamic Moors from the Iberian Peninsula that would culminate in 1492 under the Catholic Monarchs Isabella and Ferdinand.
6   Term used to indicate European foreigners to the north of present-day Spain. Literally interpreted as "beyond the mountains," which in this case meant beyond the Pyrenees.
7   "Arias Moragas, caballero catalán, se halló con gente de Aragón y de Navarra en la Batalla de las Navas de Tolosa" - http://www.blasonari.net/apellido.php?id=679
8   "Quienes quisieron saquear en el campo encontraron muchas cosas, oro, por supuesto plata, preciosos vestidos, materiales de seda y muchos otros adornos valiosísimos, y ciertamente mucho dinero y vasos valiosos, de lo que todo en su mayor parte se apoderaron los infantes y otros soldados de Aragón." - http://www.bajoaragonesa.org/elagitador/la-batalla-de-las-navas-de-tolosa-i-cronica-de-rodrigo-jimenez-de-rada/
9   Llul p. 66
10 Mostly Hospitalers and Templars

11 Isabella and Ferdinand
12 North and South American continents
13 "It must also be borne in mind that inquisitors and their staffs were not only agents of a persecutory spiritual tribunal, but also were likely to be knowledgeable and well-connected members of the local elites among whom they resided. As such, they were sometimes drawn into legal and financial conflicts that might have little to do with the business of inquisition *per se*. In relatively underdeveloped settings such as colonial Peru, inquisitors' familiarity with legal and religious affairs may have made their intervention all the more desirable for clerical or university colleagues dealing with complex financial issues such as the execution of a will or a bankruptcy." - https://inquisition.library.nd.edu/
14 Barletta p. 76
15 Carr p. 157
16 Lea p. 112
17 Carr p. 259
18 This behavior among Catholic clergy was not rare at this time. Church policies involving masculinity and sexual conduct, though standardized, were not always strictly enforced.
19 Carr p. 25
20 This treaty essentially divided the world between Spain and Portugal in 1494 and allowed for both to establish trade route networks and settlement throughout the known world.
21 Consejo Superior de Investigaciones Cientificas Patronato Menendez Y Pelayo, Institution Gonzalo Fernandez De Oviedo, Catalogo de Pasajeros A Indias Durante Los Siglos XVI, XVII, Y XVIII p. 63
22 Higman p. 62
23 Present day island that includes the nations of Haiti and the Dominican Republic.
24 Perez Jr. pp. 3-5
25 "They ... brought us parrots and balls of cotton and spears and many other things, which they exchanged for the glass beads and hawks' bells. They willingly traded everything they owned... . They were well-built, with good bodies and handsome features.... They do not bear arms, and do not know them, for I showed them a sword,

they took it by the edge and cut themselves out of ignorance. They have no iron. Their spears are made of cane.... They would make fine servants.... With fifty men we could subjugate them all and make them do whatever we want" – Columbus. Zinn p. 1
26   Katz http://williamlkatz.com/first-american-freedom-fighter/
27   Bartolome De Las Casas was an enlightened Catholic priest who condemned the treatment and enslavement of native Caribbean tribes by the Spanish. His ideas helped to pave the way against native enslavement by the Spanish in the New World and one of the first to actively speak against it.

28   Captain Diego Martinez de Hurtaide took part in back dealings with the Mayo tribe to join the fight with
the Yaqui tribe.
29   Hrdlička p. 54
30   http://www.moragahistory.com/?page_id=59
31   Officer p. 20
32   Kellogg p. 211
33   Kellog p. 202
34   Ibid
35   Kellog p. 72
36   Many of the U.S. cities in the Southwest were also once Native American centers (or near them at least), that came under Spanish control, then Mexican, and eventually American.
37   Smith p. 6-8
38   http://anza.uoregon.edu/moraga.html
39   Even though Mexico did not exist then, it is commonly referred to as such.
40   "El reguero de muertos, cautivos, robos, incursiones, persecuciones, emboscadas y alcances continuó a lo largo del año 1792 y 1793. El rosario de incidentes menores, pero que muchas veces implicaban la pérdida de vidas humanas, era constante. Sirva de indicador del estado de inseguridad en que las incursiones apaches mantenían a las provincias bajo autoridad española la siguiente relación de incidentes que se sucedieron en la provincia de Sonora durante los meses de verano y otoño" – "Revista de Historia Militar" Instituto de historia y cultura militar Año LVI 2012 Núm. 111 p. 137

41   Ferguson, Stephen, Colwell-Chanthaphonh pp. 193-201
42   http://www.library.arizona.edu/exhibits/desertdoc/aravaipa.htm p. 60
43   This event marks the popular American holiday "Cinco De Mayo."
44   Miller p.108
45   Lindsay preface- p. x
46   An Act for the Government and Protection of Indians April 22, 1850   Chapter 133, Statutes of California, April 22, 1850
47   Civil War Data Regiment Personnel Listing
48   Battle of Picacho Pass was the furthest westward battle fought between the Union and Confederates and occurred outside of Tucson in 1862.
49   Civil War Data Regiment Personnel Listing
50   Masich p. 118
51   Dodson p. 142
52   Balderamma and Rodriguez p. 306
53   Edward Moraga in discussion with the author, August 1, 2005
54   Laslet p. 137
55   Laslet p. 138
56   Laslet p. 140
57   Rosalinda Moraga in discussion with the author, November 13, 2015 – "Family accounts point to Edward having pro-Communist pamphlets in his house."
58   Edward Moraga in discussion with the author, August 1, 2005.
59   Ibid.
60   Edward Moraga Jr. in discussion with the Author, April 16, 2017.
61   Gutierrez p. 191
62 Cherrie Moraga in discussion with author, August 31, 2015
63 Moraga p. 82
64   Cherrie Moraga in discussion with author, August 31, 2015
65   Ibid.
66   Ibid.
67   North and South American continents

68   Moraga's Pride "Rancho Laguna de los Palos Colorados" by Sandy Kimball
69   The Moraga name exists in former Spanish colonies in Asia such as the Philippines.
70   "From early post-contact times, the baptism of infants and adults were occasions on which Christian names were acquired by Native Americans." Sturtevant p. 217
71   Kimball p. 3
72   Hunt p. 3